FROM RACIST TO NON-RACIST TO ANTI-RACIST: BECOMING PART OF THE SOLUTION

FROM RACIST TO NON-RACIST TO ANTI-RACIST: BECOMING PART OF THE SOLUTION

KEITH L. ANDERSON, PHD

Contents

Acknowledgements

For my wife Jeanne and my sons Elijah and Nathan. They have had to live with the ups and downs of a man who preaches and fights against racism. Passion turns fighters for social justice into passionate warriors. Living with passionate warriors isn't always an easy task.

Thanks To:

My former writing mentors William C. Anderson (BAT21) & Kent C. Anderson (Night Dogs). I've always thought it odd that neither William C. nor Kent C. are related. Nor am I related to either one of them. Regardless of the last name coincidence, they both taught me a lot about writing.

I would also like to thank Bob Casper and Frederick Lincoln Johnson for helping me bring this book to the finish line.

About the cover:

Quilt design by Jeanne L. Anderson. Cover design and quilt photographs by Elijah L. Anderson.

Praise God, through whom all blessings flow.

Introduction

For years I've wanted to write a book about racism. But after visiting Barnes and Nobles, both online and our actual bookstore here in Boise, Idaho; I realized there were already volumes of books and articles written on the subject of racism. I asked myself, could I write a book on racism that would be different than the books already available? So, I started to think about my twenty years of personal experiences, conducting courses, giving seminars, lectures and writing articles about racism. In those seminars, lectures and articles, I always wanted to make sure my students, the attendees and readers learned something specific; something they could take home and use immediately. After realizing what I'd been doing for all those years, I decided that teaching something very specific about racism would be make my book different. In all my lectures, seminars, courses and articles, I always had a primary goal; teach people how to move from being a non-racist, to becoming an anti-racist. Everything I spoke, taught and wrote was about helping people to see where they really stood regarding racism and how to take the necessary action to becoming a positive change agent. That was it! My book will tell people how to take the action of moving from non-racist to anti-racist.

The next question was, what piece of knowledge could I give people to help them take the actions needed to move them from non-racist to anti-racist, thus, becoming positive change agents? Throughout my teaching and speaking experience I've realized something very important. Most people in America tend to hold true to what they believed and what they felt about racism; rather than the facts about racism, in America. Therefore, I would teach people an important fact about racism. I wouldn't write a dissertation about about racism. I would explore one fact about racism and teach it. So, I went back to my teachings, seminars and lectures notes and I found exactly which fact I wanted to teach in my book on racism.

I decided to teach people **the difference between a racist, a non-racist and an anti-racist.** Here's why; the lack of understanding and defining who is a racist, a non-racist and an anti-racist; has always been a dagger sticking through the heart of America. This lack of admitting, knowing, understanding and defining racism has been one of the biggest obstacles keeping America from realizing its true potential and obligation to provide equality to all its citizens. Also, the lack of admitting, knowing, understanding and defining racism is a major reason why America cannot rid itself of racism. And if America doesn't understand what racism is, and deal with it once and for all, America will eventually commit social suicide.

I believe anyone, regardless of the color of their skin, who possesses the heart and the guts and the knowledge to help America understand racism, should. In my book, since I am an educated Black man, racism will be dealt with from an educated Black man's perspective. The science of racism has been poked, prodded, observed and talked about through slavery, stealing the land from Native Indians, reconstruction, Japanese internment camps Jim Crow and the Civil Rights Movement, and yet racism still lives in America. The goal of my book will be to get everyday people to understand racism to the point, of being able to do something which could help them get rid of racism in their communities. The best way to do so, in my opinion, is to minimize the peripheral information, which causes us to talk on and on about racism. I want to give folks the knowledge to get out of their huddles and run the plays that rid our communities of racism. Therefore, my book will home in on a common-sense approach. The commonsense approach I will use entails, helping folks to learn enough about racism to be able to DO something, that will help rid their own communities of racism. If everyone used this commonsense approach of learning and applying what they've learned, communities could put a serious dent in their racism situations.

Last but certainly not least, I, as the author of this book on dealing with racism, will not be firing thoughts, like bullets, across the country at White people. I live in Idaho (since 1977), the heart of

America's whiteness. The Black population in Idaho is 1%! Therefore, I deal with some form of racism, up-close and personal, on a regular basis. I live here and fight for racial justice, with very little mental or financial support. The next section of this book will further explain my situation.

So, who will this book help? We have many important social situations going on in America. People are dealing with health-care issues. People are becoming aware that the top one percent of Americans own ninety percent of America's wealth. Americans are realizing that the American Dream has all but disappeared. But, believe me when I say, ahead of them all, is racism; and it has dominated America since the first Europeans sailed here and settled in a place and called it Jamestown in 1607. Racism is why they quickly massacred the native people. Racism allowed them to buy, steal and sell Africans into slavery. Racism was the catalyst behind forcing the Chinese to work the railroads and live in underground cities. Racism put Japanese people into internment camps and stole their property. Over the years Europeans have affectionately called these acts of racism, "pulling oneself up by ones' bootstrap". Racism, disguising itself as "pulling oneself up by ones' bootstrap", would have been more difficult to accomplish had the Europeans, now Americans, not created a government and then enlisted the help of their new governmental body, to do their bidding. Within the words of America's documents of freedom and sown within the fabric of the America's institutions and flag, is a powerful ideology called racism. It dwells smack dab in the heart of social and civic justice, education, religion, health and financial wealth. Racism continues to chug along throughout American society like a locomotive, purposely set to steamroll anyone who isn't the right color. Racism never gets fixed because Americans have been taught to not truly understand it or speak freely about it. Racism never gets fixed because anyone with a pair of lips and a tongue thinks and speaks as if their feelings are facts. Racism never gets fixed because White people think people of color are the only victims of it. Racism never gets fixed because whites in power have been able to convince poor whites, that people of color are the reason they are in the financial and social predicament they're in. Racism never gets fixed because White America doesn't invest in ridding America of racism. The bottom line is racism never gets fixed because people do not understand that racism was perpetrated on purpose, therefore it must be un-done on purpose. Racism isn't just going to go away because of a moving speech. It will take love, desire, money and White people willing to take a backseat (until they acquire real knowledge) to people of color, in regards to moving people from racist to non-racist to anti-racist. This book is intended to be an aid to moving people from racist to non-racist to anti-racist. *I am writing this book for people who want to be change agents in the area of racial justice. I am writing this book for true patriots, who want the best for America.*

This book isn't written to teach the reader about slavery, Jim Crow, Black History or the history of the civil rights movement. There are plenty of well written books, written by very dedicated and detailed historians, who can make a reader a walking wealth of historical civil rights information. Some may say, in order to fix the future, we must know and understand the past. To a certain degree, I agree. But living in the historical, can sometimes prevent action towards improving the future.

People who deal with the effects of racism, need to unite and fight. Uniting as a team, allows many people to use their skills and talents to fight against the growth of racism. On a successful team there are many people performing many duties and, at any given time any one of the people on that team can be the reason the team is successful. As a former football player, I've been in games where the kicker, often the smallest guy on the team, wins the game. In fact, playing college football taught me; knowing a play doesn't mean anything if you can't or don't run the play. And if you can't or don't run the play you'll never score. If you never score you cannot win! Fixing racism in our individual communities, will put a dent in how racism effects this country. This fight takes a mighty team effort in a game where every point will matter. My contribution to the team is: **I need to teach white people how to move from racist to non-racist to anti-racist.** It takes a special set of shoulders to do what I am suggesting. And I know there are others like myself. I am not the only one. Sadly, very few people know who people like me are because we're not famous athletes or wealthy entertainers or businesspeople. People like me are just people who understand why America has never reached its full potential. People like me know that the inner-workings and mechanics of racism has affected all Americans dearly.

Each chapter will include helpful information about an aspect of racism. Also, each chapter will include an important step on how to become an anti-racist. Another important aspect of each chapter includes short essays regarding my thoughts on racism in America. These essays will comment on racism from the aspect of several American institutions; such as education, religion, wealth and America's social climate. These essays were written to help induce the reader to engage in meaningful and thoughtful conversation about racism. Once the reader has read the contents of this book, they will be able to converse from an informative perspective rather than an emotional perspective. Just for the record, some of the sources I use are older. They are older not because I was too lazy to research newer statistics for old problems. I used older resources for two reasons. First, there are people who have been concerned about and fighting racism in education for a long time. They deserve some credit. Second, I use older resources because things still have not gotten better and I want the reader to see how long racism has been looked at in America. In fact, in many areas of education, racism continues to make the prospect of progress feel further from a possible reality.

The Cost of Freedom

by Keith L. Anderson

What we have right now is a whisper from the past
We think we're moving forward but we're still running last
There's a toll one must pay while living outside one's skin
And if we aren't careful, a slave mentality will kill our asses again
From sea to shining sea we labor behind our masks
Trying to work our way up from being treated like second class
And those in the White House have charged us a mighty cost
Because they're busy telling White folk we're the reason for their
loss
The time has come
I hope you can see
The cost of freedom
Has to be paid by you and me
It wouldn't be so bad but many angry folks, truly believe
They don't even realize, the words of a pimp will always deceive
He lies and says he's the only one with the answers and the way
So, just look deep inside your pockets there's more for you to pay
One day his followers will realize hate has ripped out their hearts
But we should not wait around for their actions to tear our lives
apart
We must come together and help each other like we never have
before
Or our freedoms will be taken and we'll be locked behind some door
The time has come
I hope you can see
The cost of freedom
Has to be paid by you and me

So Who Am I?

I think it's only fair you know who is writing to you about racism, an important stumbling block of American society. My name is Keith L. Anderson. I was born in Cleveland, Ohio but my family only stayed there until I was five months old. I did the formative years of my growing up in Vallejo, California. When I was around ten years old my father, who was into music, thought he needed to live in Los Angeles in order to "make it big" in the music business. So, he left his wife and family. I have only seen him 3 times in fifty years. This means I was raised by my Mama and her three sisters. Two of Mama's sisters lived with us for a while. That meant Mama and I, my two aunties, my brother and my three sisters, lived in a rented, small 3-bedroom house. Eventually my aunties married and moved out. Because the landlord liked how hard Mama worked to keep her family together, she made it easy for Mama to buy the house we lived in. Before I go any further, I want to share with you from where my mentality comes.

Somewhere deep inside my mind, what I really thought and felt had always been smothered. I have always kept my true thoughts in check. I think I did so because I've always been afraid of how I might react to knowing the massive amount of bullshit America had been spreading on the lives of Black people and young Black men. So, I subconsciously or maybe even consciously subdued who I really was and what I really thought. Staying within myself caused me to continually ask myself, am I angry, or, am I an intellectual starving for answers? And, will those answers ever be fed to me? Am I kind, or do I pretend? Do I long for God to be real? Constantly asking myself these questions, made me feel like someone with multiple personalities. I thought maybe one day I'd find out which of the personalities was really me. The only thing I can be sure of is, I'm not who everyone thinks I am. But there is one person I know I am. I know I'm a Black man living in America. In fact, I'm reminded of this fact by living in perhaps the whitest state in America, Idaho.

Football gave me the proper outlet to vent my anger. First it was Pop Warner football, then high school, junior college and eventually I came to Idaho as a twenty-year-old junior college transfer, on a full-ride football scholarship. Whoever I was, was quickly smothered by more than the whiteness of Idaho's snowfall. Idaho's whiteness forced me to face my blackness day to day, month to month and year in and year out. The battle between being black and being me, ended when I realized both live permanently within me. I had to make myself understand that I was more than black. I was my Mama's oldest child, a big brother, a nephew of four black women, and I was a football player. And still deeper down inside of me, Mama had also planted the seed for me to someday realize that I was a child of God.

In my blackness I have learned to understand whiteness, which is unavoidable in America. I have also learned, being angry at the whiteness I was experiencing, took away from me appreciating the totality of my blackness. I came to realize, once I knew and understood my blackness, I could be confident; that I could deal with the whiteness that surrounded me. This led to an untapped strength. Understanding the untapped strength inside of me, helped me to understand what I had to do with my life. I soon realized that blackness wasn't about talking a certain way. This meant not allowing black stereotypes to define me. I wasn't going to allow stereotypes to cause me to act the way White people said or imagined I should act. Blackness was and is about a shared understanding of perseverance, history and style. My understanding of my blackness helped me to realize that I wasn't a stepchild of civilization. I have been here since the beginning and have been a vital force within the family of man. This knowledge gives me the courage to walk into a room of White people and teach them about racism, from a Black man's perspective. This boldness allows me to not shoot sniper shots from across town or across the country at the very people who needed to hear and listen to my message up-close and personal. My blackness caused me to understand, I can only help White people by being in the same room with them; not hurling insults, coded messages or misunderstandings from behind my computer keyboard.

My first realization came when I learned, White people varied in attitude and knowledge of what racism really was and is. Within my personal experience and relationships, I can count on one hand, white people who I know, who truly care and who truly understand how racism works. I have learned that most White people I dealt with wanted to base their understanding of racism on how they felt. I can't tell you how many times what came out of their mouths was justified by how they felt, and truth be damned! As bold as my realization of blackness made me, I came to understand white feelings versus white facts, which caused me to be extra cautious with my trust. This made me sad until I rationalized that the only trust I owed anyone was to teach the truth as best as I could. The only thing I wanted from White people was a willingness to open their minds and give in to the possibility that maybe they didn't understand what they thought they understood.

I grew up poor financially but accumulated a wealth of spirit. I may not have had a father, but I had my Mama and her sisters. I had Mr. P. Graham, a black man, of the Omega Continental Boys Club. Coach B. Coley, a white man, my first football coach. I had my Uncle Cecil, a black man, who took me to Washington Playground to ball with the brothas. I had my junior varsity Coach N. Tanner, a white Mormon, and his assistant, Coach E. Williams, a black man. I had Coach F. Faucett, a black man and my track coach. I had Mr. D. Williams, a black man, who was not only a teacher who told me that I was a leader, not a follower; he also balled, with the brothas, down at Washington Playground. I had Coach J. Renfro, a white man, and my high school varsity football coach. I had my junior college football coach S. Wilkerson, a black man, who pulled me aside and yelled at me about a cheap-shot I took in a game. I had, at the university level Coach J. Criner and Coach D. Campo, both white men, who helped me see the link that connected football and life. At my first job after graduating college and before going to graduate school, I had A. Gaines, a black man who taught me about being a black man in the corporate world. I had Dr. M. Oliver, a black woman, a professor and eventually my pastor. I had Dr. Y. Takeda, an Asian man, who looked at one writing assignment and told me I would perhaps be a writer someday. I had Dr. M. Gardiner, a white woman who guided me to my doctorate. Last, but certainly not least, every fighter of racism needs someone in their life, who knows the lay of the land. Every fighter of racism needs someone with whom he or she can bounce around ideas, theories and thoughts. For me, that was my former college classmate, friend, fellow fighter and excellent debater, Shannon D. Work, Esq., a Native Indian. Rest in peace my brother.

All the people I mentioned are the reason I can't stomach racism. God sent all these people into my life. My job was to listen to them and take away something useful; something that I could use to do battle. I now take the tools these people put into my life and I try to share them with all the people who cross my path. These people helped me to get an associate degree in Journalism; a bachelor's degree in Human Communication; study at the Masters' level Human Communication. Their words haunted me until I earned a doctorate in Educational Leadership, at 50 years of age. My dissertation, "Teacher Communication with Students from Diverse Backgrounds" won presentations two years at the AERA Conferences in both 2006 and 2007. I've written over 150 newspaper and magazine articles on racism in religion, society and education. For 18 years, I've written, designed and taught college courses entitled Disassembling Racism, Sociology of African Americans, Speech and Multicultural Communication. I have conducted countless seminars, workshops and lectures on racism and anti-racism.

But, through all of the ugliness of racism, I have seen, and experienced tiny pieces of what America could be if we only cared more about each other. I don't know if we'll ever get all the way to the 'Promised Land', especially on a long-term basis, but if racial equality isn't worth the long fight, I don't know what is. All the previously mentioned people helped prepare me to live in a state that is only 1% Black. They helped prepare me to fight, in my own way, for racial equality. These are just a few of the things that make me qualified to teach people how to go from racist to non-racist to anti-racist. Every day I'm either learning from others or teaching others, how to fight against racism. I learn a lot from what others write, and by living in Idaho, I experience or observe racism up close and personal almost every day. Living in Idaho has taught me to fight against racism in a way that gives people insight. I try to give them an understanding of racism that will allow them to become anti-racist warriors.

Below is Idaho's population's racial breakdown:

Race	Population	% of Total
Total Population	1,567,582	100
White	1,396,487	89
Hispanic or Latino	175,901	11
Some Other Race	79,523	5
Two or More Races	38,935	2
American Indian	21,441	1
Asian	19,069	1
Black or African American	9,810	Below 1%
Three or more races	2,362	Below 1%
Native Hawaiian Pacific Islander	2,317	Below 1%
Native Hawaiian	637	Below 1%
Alaska Native tribes	403	Below 1%

(Source: suburbanstats.org 2015-2016)

Chapter One: Ist Step to Becoming an Anti-Racist

What is Racism?

Webster's New World Dictionary and Thesaurus defines racism as, "the practice of racial discrimination, segregation, etc." Google Dictionary defines racism as, "prejudice, discrimination, or antagonism directed against someone of a different race based on the belief that one's own race is superior." The People's Institute for Survival and Beyond, an organization that teaches people to un-do racism by conducting anti-racism courses, seminars and workshops, all over the world, defines racism as, "race prejudice + power = racism". I agree with each of these definitions. But for a second I'd like to focus on the definition used by 'The People's Institute for Survival and Beyond', especially the use of the word 'power'. Power is a very important term within their definition. Without "power" racism can only perpetrate a shadow of its purpose. I want to take defining racism a step further, but at the same time please remember "power" is also an important element of the racism, I'm about to introduce. But first, I want to explain racism this way.

The year is 2019 and racism has yet to be undone in America. The curiosity in regard to why racism hasn't been undone has been a constant echo ringing in the minds of the victims of racial injustice, since the taking of American soil from the Native people and the promise of forty acres and a mule to former negro slaves. Since Native Indians will not be getting their land back anytime soon and since reparation for descendants of Africa slaves has yet to come to fruition, we must focus on dealing with and eliminating racism and its manifestations. When I say we, I mean the victims of racism. At the same time, we must show an American society which will not allow the stench of racism to evanesce into a time that once was; that racism has an internal negative effect on the perpetrators, as well as on the recipients. This negative effect causes a void in the souls and conscience of racist people; a void which they feel can be filled by seeing themselves better that people from other ethnic groups.

However, in order to adequately address this country's racial dilemma, one must identify and agree upon, a working definition of racism. The definition of racism must include elements which will explain how racism works. The elements within the definition of racism must also be varied and interchangeable. At the same time the elements within the definition of racism must be so succinct, that any missing and defined element, renders the definition and any given racist act, impotent.

Neither racism nor the effects of racism are constant. This means, racism is not perpetrated and received in the same way, in each racist situation or system. This is because each racist situation or system is different and consists of different, but identifiable elements. Together, all the defined elements of racism make each particular racist situation effective. Therefore, undoing racism isn't about eliminating any single element within a racist situation or system. Undoing racism is about recognizing which element(s) are currently being used in the current racist situation or system and eliminating said element(s). There is no single miracle blanket that can be thrown over a racist situation or system that will totally smother its effects. Again, the most effective way to deal with racism, whether it is perpetrated systemically or individually, is to identify, confront and curtail the elements racist systems and racist people use. There are several systemic and individual varieties of racism which allow racism to continue and during certain times in society flourish.

Do you remember Smokey Bear?

According to Smokeybear.com there are three elements needed for a fire to occur. And if Smokey Bear doesn't know the elements of a fire, no one does. **Heat** – A heat source is responsible for the initial ignition of fire and is also needed to maintain the fire and enable it to spread. Heat allows fire to spread by drying out and preheating nearby fuel and warming surrounding air. **Fuel** – Fuel is any kind of combustible material. It's characterized by its moisture content, size, shape, quantity and the arrangement in which it is spread over the landscape. The moisture content determines how easily it will burn. **Oxygen** – Air contains about 21 percent oxygen, and most fires require at least 16 percent oxygen content to burn. Oxygen supports the chemical processes that occur during fire. When fuel burns, it reacts with oxygen from the surrounding air, releasing heat and generating combustion products (gases, smoke, embers, etc.). This process is known as oxidation.

Like the elements needed to start a fire, there are also elements needed for racism to exist. According to the definitions of racism we mentioned earlier, the elements of racism must be ignited by those with power. And like the elements needed for fire, those with power must control certain elements for racism to be perpetrated successfully and continued on an ongoing basis. Contrary to popular belief, racism isn't caused by hatred. Hatred is a manifestation of racism and can be used as fuel to sustain racism. The act of racism is caused by one powerful group of people using their access to certain elements, to control another group of people with less or no power. So, what are the elements of racism?

Introducing the Anderson Hypothesis of Explaining Racism

The Anderson Hypothesis of Explaining Racism states: When a nation's more economically, politically powerful and entitled race or culture assigns and attaches internal superiority, un-true history, while deleting the use of sound reasoning based on scientific knowledge, historical fact and meaningful communication; to the politically and economically powerless people within its society, racism will occur and remain constant.

The observance of truth, through scientific knowledge, historical facts, the relinquishing of an internalized superiority complex and the attitude of entitlement, must replace, the dominant culture perpetuating an atmosphere of internal superiority and untrue history, which is being referred to these days as, "alternative facts". Sound reasoning, based on scientific knowledge, historical fact and meaningful communication, must become the norm, or racism will continue to exist.

As I look at the history of racism in the United States, I am convinced my hypothesis on racism can be displayed as a social formula. I see the social formula for racism stated as such: If IS= internal superiority; UH= un-true history; EC&PPE=economic and political power and entitlement; is greater than KF= knowledge & facts; MCOM=Meaningful communication; R =racism will occur and remain constant. If (IS+UH)(EC&PPE) directed negatively towards a particular racial group > (KF +MCOM) R will occur and remain constant.

Reasoning for formula: If ((IS+UH)(EC&PPE)>(KF+MCOM))=R

If economic power, and a feeling of superiority, over people from a non-power race or group of people, disregarding accurate knowledge and facts about said non-power race or group of people occurs; racism will prevail and remain constant. Therefore, should the American people continue to not engage in meaningful, knowledgeable and factual communication about race and racism, racism will continue to exist.

Formula scope:

If America continues to allow a group of people to practice internal superiority and untrue history, falsely produced because they are more economically and politically powerful, and they have the means to use their innate feelings of entitlement; over the economically and politically powerless races or groups of people, rather than using sound reasoning based on scientific knowledge, historical fact and meaningful communication; racism will prevail and remain constant.

Formula explained:

If internal superiority and untrue history, about people from a particular race or group of people, by a race or group of people who are more economically, politically powerful and entitled, is greater than sound reasoning, based on knowledge, fact and meaningful communication; racism will occur and remain constant. ***Eliminate any part(s) of the (greater than, elements of this formula), systemic and individual acts of racism as we know them, cannot function and will eventually cease to exist.*** In other words, just like taking an element away from what causes a fire, extinguishes the fire, eliminate any part or parts of the elements of racism as it is defined above and it cannot logically survive.

Racism isn't about hate:

As you can see racism does not need hatred in order to exist. People often perpetrate racism with a smile on their faces. Therefore, hatred isn't the cause of racism. In fact, hate is merely one result produced by racism. Racism also produces internalized superiority complex, which applied correctly to powerless people, creates within the powerless an internalized inferiority complex. Being a victim of either of these conditions doesn't necessarily create hatred. It does however create a lopedsided system in which the powerful always inflict pain and anguish onto the powerless.

Fighting racism:

So, what are we to do in our fight to rid America of its racism? We must stop allowing racist people to keep us fighting useless battles with Don Quixote's windmills. We must rid the racist of the real elements which allow the manifestations of racism to systematically metastasize throughout educational, religious, political and economic systems, government and private institutions and, the mindset within cultures and individuals.

White People's Role in Fighting Racism:

My knowledge and experience in teaching anti-racism is often discounted by Whites. It is discounted because of what Joseph Barndt says in 'Understanding & Dismantling Racism: The twenty-first Century Challenge to White People', "As White people who participate in multiracial coalitions and organizations, we must learn two hard lessons. One is the ability to follow the leadership of people of color. This is very hard for us, since it is at the very core of racism that whites should lead and people of color follow. Second, if we no longer lead, it is hard to avoid the opposite temptation: to stand on the sidelines and limit our participation to mere cheering. We are not just supporters of people of color, but co-participants in this struggle for the freedom of us all. Eliminating racism is an equal opportunity task that welcomes all participants (Barndt, 1991 p. 163; 2007 p. 228)."

My experiences in seminars and workshops have been overwhelmingly difficult. Because of Barndt's statement above, trying to train white folk about racism and anti-racism continues to be a task not meant for people who are thin-skinned. Most of the time, the defensiveness in the room, is so thick, it could be cut with a knife. I often had to work extra hard to gain White people's trust. Most do not like getting their bubble busted about their rights to their feelings and how I must value their opinions. For them it is difficult to replace feelings and opinions with historical facts and statistical truths. However, I have seen the lightbulb pop on over the heads of more than a few attendees. Seeing the light bulb pop on in someone is what gives trainers the motivation, desire and energy to continue anti-racism work.

Essay #1. Racism Aches In Me Deeply

My soul is tired, and my eyes run like a river. Violence and hatred uncontrollably spin this country. Its shear force throws this society so far off course that we will never again be centered enough to love, live and let live. I ache deeply, like a hopeless romantic watching a sad movie. But this isn't a movie. It's living color, on a stage that has become black and white. As a youngster growing up in Vallejo, California, my Mama taught me to treat everyone the same. She often reminded me that good and bad came in all shapes, sizes and colors. As an adult I've tried living my life as a beacon of racial peace and harmony. However, I'm not a wealthy star athlete, famous rapper or an actor. No one cares what I think. Still, I'm compelled to pass on a piece of knowledge.

If this country treated everyone with respect, there would be no need for "Black Lives Matter". And even if one person doesn't deserve respect, don't lay that person's ignorance on a whole race, culture or group of people. "Black Lives Matter" is important because right now in this country Black people are being killed. For Black People this is real, and it breaks our hearts. Therefore, we must scream "Black Lives Matter". Black people can be killed so freely, that an internalized inferiority complex has become prevalent in the subconscious of many Black people, especially young Black men. However, every time we try to bring this serious situation to the forefront of society, people want to water it down by coming up with things like, "All Lives Matter" or "Blue Lives Matter". Only a heartless individual would not understand that all and blue lives matter. However, "Black Lives Matter" is a cry for inclusion within the belief that "All Lives Matter". Stop killing Black people as if we don't matter. Stop mistreating Black people as if we don't matter. If this country can't see and be honest about its racism and hatred problem, then we have no choice but to believe that racism and hatred are being perpetrated and ignored on purpose.

One day I had lunch with Shannon Work, a friend I've known since college, who happens to be Native Indian. He's a lawyer who has argued in front of the United States Supreme Court (I was so proud of him.). He explained to me the Native perspective regarding respecting Mother Earth. I totally agreed with what he was saying. But my experience has been, if man can't respect his fellow man, he ain't gonna give a damn about the ozone layer, trees, recycling or anything else, that is good for our environment. I told him, I'll start worrying about recycling, when I have don't have to worry about my Black teenaged sons being shot over a broken taillight. I'll be concerned about global warming when White people can no longer call the police and have them harass me, just because I'm sitting in a park, minding my own business.

Throughout history Black people have had to desperately scream, "Black Lives Matter". We hold these truths to be self-evident, that all men are created equal. The truth of the matter is Negroes had to scream "Black Lives Matter" even back when The Constitution was written, in order to have a special amendment added, because those great words of The Constitution didn't include the Negro. In fact, many of the men who wrote those great words went back to their plantations and the slaves they owned. Today, just by virtue of being an American, Black people shouldn't ever have to scream "Black Lives Matter". But the power of racism, dictates that Black people better scream as loud as possible, "Black Lives Matter".

Racism's system of power is so well imbedded in our society, Black folk throughout history have always had to scream and fight against it. Nevertheless, there is one element of racism that is vital to its existence. When people aren't educated, they can be subjected to any treatment a racist system decides to dish out. I use the word 'decides', because racism is never an accident. It is done on purpose and therefore it must be un-done on purpose. To rid this country of racism it will take more than people feeling sad towards horrible, racist acts. It will take direct and deliberate actions and move from non-racist to anti-racist. This country will have to deal with racism in a very deliberate way, because this country's apathy and systematic killing of young Black folks' minds, via an educational system that is full of White teachers who have little to no training in the area of racism; continues to kill as many young Blacks as the guns of policemen and racists. This is disheartening. And with all my heart, I wish my words mattered. So, I often wonder, where are our Black heroes? Hell, I'll even take some White heroes. Where are those anti-racist people who really want to make society a better place? I work, helping low income students and students of all colors, get into college. I was put on this planet to enrich, not get rich. Who knows, maybe one of them will be the next Dr. King or Cesar Chavez.

As I peer out into America's society, I am confused, much like Plato's Allegory of the Cave. Are we real or are we merely shadows of what man is supposed to be? But I am brought back from the shadows, to reality, by the trails of blood and bodies. And yes, having to work so hard to navigate my way through the shadows of racism oftentimes makes me feel like giving up. But the memory of those before me, who fought so hard and died so senselessly, in hopes of creating a day when the land of milk and honey would flow to each man or woman based on the mere fact they are human, prevents me from giving up. So, the piece of knowledge I share with you is, please do not try to make sense of society's hatred. Don't waste time peering into hatred's cave trying to discern if racism is real. Rather, in your own personal society, make definite plans to curtail the hatred perpetrated by racism. And just maybe, before the stage dims, we might begin to feel what being human is truly about. And let's hope, that if we work hard enough, we won't need to cry "Black Lives Matter". But until then, we understand that "Black Lives Matter" at its core, is a serious desire for equal inclusion into the United States of America family.

Essay #2. The Magic of Racism

A good magician knows the art of deception. A great magician can make an audience see and believe something most intelligent people know isn't and never could be real. For instance, we all know that a person can't be sawed in half and put back together. Yet, as an audience we actually believe it's possible. What's really going on is just a sleight of hand and intentional misdirection. Racism, which is race prejudice plus power, is much like magic. Racism needs the power to intentionally misdirect what's truly going on. Without the power to intentionally misdirect what's truly going on, racism becomes impotent. The intentional misdirection of racism is designed to keep its victims from seeing and understanding what is really going on. An example of this would be Black-on-Black crime. When Black people start talking about making things better, racism does a sleight of hand and brings up Black-on-Black crime. I know Black-on-Black crime exists. According to Blackdemographics.com the 2013 US Census Bureau estimated that there are 45,003,665 African Americans in the United States which means that only 14.1% of the total American population, which numbers at 316.1 Million. However, this country is 67-70% White. Which means that 211.7 Million to 221.7 Million are White. All one must do is read the newspaper or watch the news and you'll understand that there is robbing, stealing and even killings in White neighborhoods happening every day. Now here's the first step to the sleight of hands and misdirection magic of racism. It's not called a White-on-White crime problem. I live in a state that has only about a 20% minority population and only 1% of that minority population is Black. And just like in other states people here are victims of crimes. People here get killed. Banks here get robbed. There are home invasions. Unfortunately, there are rapes here also. Because of the population's demographics here, most of the time those crimes are White-on-White crimes. However, I've never seen or heard these crimes reported as White-on-White crime. There are poor, low income and even uneducated Whites that also live here, but I've never heard them being told to stop the White-on-White crime, before they can prosper. They are instead told that their problems are because of people of color. Most of them can go days, even weeks and not speak to a person of color, yet they believe the racist lie.

The second step to the sleight of hands and misdirection of racism, is getting Black people to believe that somehow the racism perpetrated across this country is our fault. Racists try to make us think that somehow racism would miraculously stop if there were no Black-on-Black crimes. Ridding society of racism against any group of people should not be based on what goes on in their neighborhoods. We need to stop racism because we're equally human, and it is morally wrong. And yes, there's no doubt about it, crime in Black communities needs to stop. But this country needs to stop lying about racism's cause. There would not be some kind of positive, automatic chain reaction, ridding this country of racism, if Black-on-Black crime didn't exist. Remember what happened in Tulsa, Oklahoma on June 1, 1921? Black Wall Street, the name fittingly given to one of the most affluent all-Black communities in America, was bombed from the air and burned to the ground by mobs of envious Whites. In a period spanning fewer than 12 hours, a once thriving Black business district in northern Tulsa lay smoldering – a model community destroyed and a major African-American economic movement resoundingly defused. The night's carnage left some 3,000 African Americans dead and over 600 successful businesses lost. Among these were 21 churches, 21 restaurants, 30 grocery stores and two movie theaters, plus a hospital, a bank, a post office, libraries, schools, law offices, 1500 homes, a half dozen private airplanes and even a bus system. As could have been expected, the impetus behind it all was the infamous Ku Klux Klan, working in consort with ranking city officials and many other sympathizers (SFBayview.com). The power aspect of racism kept this American atrocity and many others like it, out of the mainstream public education history books. Those African Americans people were doing what White racist people often cry. They were sticking with their own kind and prospering. This was the ultimate case of damn if you do, damn if you don't.

While we're focusing on the lie, Black-on-Black crime, our children aren't receiving the same level of education as their White counterparts. Black-on-Black crime kills the body and robs us, and it needs to stop. However, the magical power of institutional racism kills the future, one generation at a time, forever.

There are millions of Black people who believe 'Black Lives Matter' because we want to be counted in 'All Lives Matter' and we haven't been. However, the intentional misdirection power of racism would have you believe that because a few militant Black people might mean something negative, that all hard-working Black people must also mean something negative when they want Black lives to matter. Just like the person who gets sawed in half by the magician, non-thinking people, even though logic dictates that they shouldn't, believe Black people really think and believe only our lives matter. Americans needs to focus on the hidden hand, which hides the power and the magician of racism. That is the hand secretly killing us all.

Chapter Two. 2nd Step to Becoming An Anti-Racist

2nd Step to becoming an anti-racist: You must understand what a racist person is.

What is a racist?

Again, I must remind you, hatred isn't the cause of racism. In fact, hatred is merely one result produced by the elements of racism. Therefore, an important fact to remember is, racists don't have to hate the subject of their racism, in order to do harm or injustice. Also be reminded that my purpose is to point out enough about racism, so you'll know it when you see it; and you'll have the knowledge to un-do racism in your personal environment. Personally, I believe there is only one race; that's humans. In my sometimes-naive description of what I think the world should be like, everyone is part of the race of humans. When I say everyone, I mean that includes every man, woman and child, regardless of the color of their skin. Defining the humans as a race should be a no brainer. However, race and racism in America is more complicated than skin color. Like I mentioned earlier, when it comes to talking about racism and race and how we view ourselves in relationship to racism, our feelings and our rights to our opinions have caused the facts regarding race and racism to get lost in the mix. When it comes to racism, most people fall under one of the following perspectives. It doesn't matter whether you are an individual, a company or corporation, or an institution; you are **racist, non-**

racist or anti-racist. There is a very distinctive difference between these three perspectives.

Racist People

A racist person uses their race-based powers to mistreat people based on their race or as in America, skin color. **A racist person** uses his or her race-based powers to control and/or destroy the lives of people who do not have the same color skin he or she has. **A racist person** believes their own race is superior to all other races. **A racist person** either doesn't believe or doesn't acknowledge facts which disprove the beliefs of superiority. This means they often misinterpret facts to fit their beliefs. Stick with me on this point, white racist and racists of color are not the same. To be honest, according to our definition of racism, people of color aren't and can't be truly racist. They can be prejudiced, mean or hateful. However, people of color normally don't possess, except in very rare occasions, the 'power' it takes to be a true racist. This country doesn't give people of color the power to be true racists. Yes, there are a few wealthy Black people who, from the outside, look as though they have power, but, they have very little, if any. On the physical level someone of color may possess temporary power over a less physical White person. But that power is quickly extinguished when the law gets involved. In the past few years, we have seen White people use their power to call the police on people of color and especially Black people. They do so for the obvious reason of having the power to do so.

Many times, in situations which involve the police, Black people and people of color don't have the sustaining power of law enforcement on our side. In a lot of the cases made public where a White person calls the police on a Black person or person of color, the Black person or person of color isn't doing anything wrong. However, the White person knows the dangerous possibilities in which a Black person or person of color can find themselves when the police are called. Anyone who doesn't understand this danger, is either lying, or they aren't playing with a full deck. White people who do this get the satisfaction of watching the police wrestle Black folk or people of color to the ground or worse. Therefore, calling the police on black people or people of color, has become popular. It satisfies the ego of racists and gives them a sense of superiority and power. Because America doesn't train law enforcement well enough in the area of racism, and because a lot of law enforcement officers have biases against people of color, racist civilians know they can set it up so law enforcement can hurt or kill black people or people of color. If neither police, nor the lying white racist, must pay any consequences for their actions, this form of racism will continue. Mean or hateful people of color don't have enough power to pull off this brand of execution. Racist people must be part of a racist system for racism to work. If the systems operating in America didn't accept or associate with racist acts, racism would not be able to operate or exist as it does.

Here's an example of how racism works and how white people's power trumps the legal innocence of Black people. It also proves why people of color aren't truly racists. In March 2019, a black woman called 911 and the police ended up wrestling her to the ground. Here's the story as written in an article, in *Slate Magazine*, written by Molly Olmstead:

A South Florida police officer has been suspended after a video circulated on social media showing him putting a black woman in a headlock after she called to report a crime, according to local media reports.

Dyma Loving has said she had called 911 on March 5 after getting into an argument with her neighbor, who waved a shotgun at her. She told reporters later that the neighbor had called her and her friend "whores." She said the two had ignored it at first, but her friend, Adrianna Green, eventually threw a potted plant toward the neighbor's yard. The neighbor, a white man, then allegedly pulled out a shotgun and said he would "shoot my burnt black-ass face off my neck," she told the Miami New Times.

When police showed up, they interviewed the two women. One officer, later identified by the department as Alejandro Giraldo, "started interrogating us like we were the suspects," Loving told the New Times. Loving said she asked him if she could go to her friend's house to charge her phone and call her children. "He kept telling me I needed to calm down, but I was so scared at that moment," she told the New Times.

In the video, which was filmed by Green and appears to start after she asks Giraldo to go to her friend's house, one of the officers can be heard saying, "she needs to be corrected if anything." Loving, visibly upset, asks the police officers, "Why do I have to be corrected when my life was just threatened and my daughter's sick? I just want to go to the store to charge my phone."

Giraldo takes a step toward her. He then seizes her arm and appears to push her toward the fence behind her as Green protests that she hadn't done anything.

Loving repeatedly tells the officers not to touch her, and as another officer holds her wrists, Giraldo forcefully tries to handcuff her. Loving, though shouting does not appear to physically resist. Then, Giraldo yanks his arm away, and—as Green repeatedly cries out, "Why are you doing this?"—places her in a headlock and wrestles her to the ground. The three officers then pin her to the ground.

The Black woman in this situation wasn't a racist. I brought up her situation to show why a person of color would find it difficult to be a true racist. We don't have the sustaining power of law enforcement on our side. The man pointing the gun at these Black women had all the power, simply by virtue of having white skin. He got the satisfaction of watching the police wrestle her to the ground. This is the reason calling the police on people of color, has become so popular. It satisfies the ego of racists.

Racist companies, corporations, churches,

government, media and the educational system

Because of the power to legislate, interpret and implement rules and laws; governments, politicians and institutions such as companies, corporations, churches and the educational system can also be racist. This is called systemic racism. The people who run or work for the government, politicians and institutions such as companies, corporations, churches and the educational system are mostly White people. These entities employ individuals, who might not have a lot of power, but because they represent the government, politicians and institutions such as companies, corporations, churches and the educational system; they can perpetrate racism with protection of the powerful people who run these entities.

Racism in companies and corporations

Racism in companies and corporations is oftentimes difficult to prove. Black people and people of color not getting raises or promotions can be and often are refuted by supervisors proclaiming attitudinal problems. And, unless White people are willing to reveal their income, a Black person or people of color never really know if he or she is being paid the same wages as their white counterparts. Nowadays, there are so many other injustices going on in companies and corporations, racism seems to have banished to the far corners of the human resources files.

There's a very slick, but very visible weapon companies and corporations use to perform their racism. Because Black people and people of color can spot this not so secret weapon in a New York second, it oftentimes tells us a lot about the company. In fact, the very visible weapon is a person, who Black people and people of color call 'the spook by the door'. I wonder what the official name the company gives this person. This person is usually a person of color that White people in the company or corporation trust. This 'spook by the door' job is to keep out other people of color. Therefore, they are normally in a position of power, in the hiring process. This person of color is carrying out the duties like a white racist would do. But how can you claim a company is racist, when the person doing the hiring is a Black person or a person of color? This is one of the reasons this act within systemic racism works so well. It's like magic.

Essay #3. Standing Rock, Racism, and Greed at its Best

I support the Standing Rock Sioux Tribe's right to protect their water today, tomorrow and fifty years down the road. However, make no doubt about it. This is racism and greed at its best, or should I say, at its worst. When Bismarck, the Capitol of North Dakota told Energy Transfer Partners to go build their pipeline somewhere else, because the venture would jeopardize the integrity of their drinking water, the Texas oil company re-routed. Here's why Bismarck could make such a demand; The racial makeup of the Bismarck is 92.4% White, 0.7% African American, 4.5% Native American, 0.6% Asian, 0.3% from other races, and 1.5% from two or more races. Hispanic or Latino of any race was 1.3% of the population (Wikipedia). Here's why Energy Transfer could not give a damn about the Standing Rock Sioux Tribe making the same request as the citizens in and around Bismarck. 4,044 – Total Population on Standing Rock Reservation (ND side only) [Census 2000]; 3,492 or 84.1% – American Indians on Standing Rock Reservation (ND side only) [Census 2010]. The perfect storm for white greed = a small number of people of color + the possibility of white people making a profit + media control = we will do whatever we have to do to take this from you. This has been a trait throughout the history of this country. This country has made and broken over 500 treaties with Native Tribes.

I'm not going to make this a history lesson about the relationship between America and the Indian Nations. That's because it can be summed up simply as lies, betrayal and greed covered up by another lie. For the Standing Rock Sioux Tribe this is about honor. For in the history of every downtrodden people, there comes a time when they must stand, sit, sing and scream in order to be heard. They must fight against the wealth of the white man and the deaf ears of a nation turned against them. They must understand, this fight will be forever, because the soul of the wealthy was long ago replaced by the glitter of gold. The brightness of gold blinds the eyes; and man can no longer see the needs of our fellow man.

In 1980 John Trudell, a Santee Sioux said, "We must go beyond the arrogance of human rights. We must go beyond the ignorance of civil rights. We must step into the reality of natural rights because all the natural world has a right to existence. We are only a small part of it. There can be no trade-off." For a while I couldn't get into what he was saying and then it hit me. One man should never have to fight another man, for human rights or civil rights. It truly goes against the natural order of the human experience. When the rights of man interfere with the profits of corporations and the skin color of the man fighting for his rights is darker than the man from the corporation, Most of the time the outcome has nothing to do with what's right.

Because one race of people owns the media, they have been able to keep the details of what is really happening at Standing Rock out of the mainstream. They show only what benefits them. They only report what is sensational and brings ratings. For those in the media who aren't under the control of the very people who would profit from this pipeline, this situation just isn't sexy enough, or violent enough. The reason it isn't sexy or violent enough is because the Sioux Tribes are trying to protest peacefully. They are trying to appeal to the common sense of the people of this country. But common sense isn't and hasn't ever been common when race and profits are on the opposite sides of the table. But despite the results of the elections several weeks ago, I have to believe, most people, if they knew the details of Standing Rock, would not approve. Again, this is about rich folks making themselves richer, by trying to bully those with the least power. However, regardless of Energy Transfer Partners and their cronies' efforts to suppress the truth, everyday more and more people are discovering the lies and injustices being perpetrated at Standing Rock.

Essay #4. A Rose by Any Other Name Would Smell As Sweet

What did William Shakespeare mean when he penned, "A rose by any other name would smell as sweet"? He meant you could call a rose, a toilet, but it wouldn't change how sweet the rose smelled. Meaning that the rose is a rose no matter what anyone decides to call it. Shakespeare was trying to bestow upon us, the knowledge that something is what it is. And no matter whatever we decide to call something, it doesn't change what it is. Well Willy Shakes, we in this country totally disagree with your correct logic. You see we've gone from "sticks and stones may break my bones, but words will never hurt me" to "you are what I call you and what I call you will break you and keep you down". We do this because we totally understand that the ability to name is power. We know that words can incite feelings good and bad. In fact, words can be used to convince one group of people to hate and even kill another group of people solely based on what words are used to describe them. We know all these things and we use it to our advantage.

It has come to my attention we the people of this country are more likely to believe what is said about people, religions and cultures, rather than research information about these people for ourselves. In other words, we want to be told what to think. Probably because it's easier to live in a reality that someone makes for us, than to create a reality based on what we've found to be true. Sadly, this way of *not* thinking has caused all kinds of problems in America. Most of the results from these problems are perpetrated on the poor, those with no power; and this country's personal favorite scapegoat–people of color. Can you say racism? I would wager that most of the racism in this country happens because of not only because of misinformation, but also undiscovered information. The people controlling mainstream knowledge, or the dissemination of knowledge are the ones shaping Americans' realities. Most of what we think we know has been filtered through the system of those in power.

I taught human communication for over 18 years at the university level. I have also designed and taught college courses on racism. I want to bring both schools of knowledge together, to show what has been done to us in America. This is for sure a very simplified version of race, reality, images and words, but I think it will make my point. The other ingredient that aids in helping to control how we think or feel, is the feeling of not possessing what we think we should possess. This becomes especially powerful when we're told that another group of people has what we're supposed to have.

One school of thought I taught students dealt with how language is only symbolic, but we allow people to give it the power to shape our realities. In other words, the words we use are an important aspect, which dictate how we view reality and our lives. So, if you want to control a person or a group of people, take control of how they view life. If you want to take control of how a person or group of people views life, tell them what to think. To tell them what to think, control the words and the images they use to describe life. The logic almost goes in a circular form, but not quite. Nevertheless, it works on people or groups of people. This is how advertisers get us to buy things we really don't need. Politicians get us to vote for them, even though they won't and in most cases can't possibly make good of their promises. But they learn to tell us what we want to hear.

Now let's look at language and how it has helped cause a nation to stay in the reality of racism. The words used to describe events are dissected and analyzed before we hear them on the news or see them in the newspaper. For instance, someone sat down and decided, let's publish the smiling, handsome picture of this young man when we report on the White male student who raped an unconscious female student. Putting this smiling picture out to the public was designed to produce positive words and thoughts about this male student (rapist). It's called "framing" and I'll explain it later.

One politician wants the President of the United States to say that the horrible murderous act perpetrated in Orlando, Florida was done by "Radical Islamists". Using this phrase attacks a very large religious group, for doing something one crazed radical individual did. If this sounds familiar, it's because in this country we are experts at naming, blaming, labeling and even condemning entire races and cultures, based on the actions of a very few or even one person. By this logic every white guy who disagrees with the things our government does should be suspected of being a potential Timothy McVeigh. Of course, that doesn't really make any sense, but racism never makes sense. Just in case no one noticed, both mentioned cowardly, terrorist acts were perpetrated by people born in America. These people are called domestic terrorists. Sadly, we are becoming very familiar with the term domestic terrorists.

"Framing" is a term news people use to decide from what angle they want a story to be seen or understood. It's used to control how the readers or viewers think. Remember the news stories of the O.J. Simpson trial? Major magazines printed pictures of O.J. and in those pictures, he was presented as dark skinned as Wesley Snipes. O.J. has lighter brown skin. Someone decided to frame that picture like that because darker Black men look scarier. If a Black person looks scary White folks think he or she must be guilty. There is a lot White on White crime committed in this country. However, we don't hear the news people framing "white on white crime". I've never heard a newscaster say, "Another murder today, as White on White crime continues to climb." But we all know about Black on Black crime. This is one-way racism slowly introduced to our realities, starting at very young ages, therefore shaping our minds, without us even knowing it is happening.

Here's an example I use when I'm talking with an audience. Years ago, I ran into an old friend from my days in banking. She was a teller who happens to be a White female. She was born and raised in Idaho. She had hit on a little bad luck. She had gotten divorced and still working her low-paying teller job, while trying to support her kids. She needed help. She wanted to make sure that her kids could see a doctor when they needed to. She went to the Health and Welfare folks, and in their wisdom, they told her- and this is according to her- if she would quit her job, they could help her. Now that was stupid advice. But what came out of her mouth next was even more stupid. She looked me in the face and said that if she was Black, they would just give her what she needed. This was in Idaho! Idaho has a Black population of 1%! Of all the Black folks I know, I couldn't think of anyone who didn't have a college degree. I couldn't think of any Black folks on welfare! So, I told her that I was willing to bet my paycheck that we could go stand outside the Health and Welfare office for a week and not see one Black person go in for help. She got upset at me. Truth hurts.

So, where did this otherwise nice woman get her racist thinking? She got it from words and images on television as she was growing up. The words and images on television news about welfare reform were drummed into her head, every evening. Forget the fact that she lived in a city where there was absolutely no way she ever experienced a disproportionate number of Blacks on welfare. Yet, she had formed her one-sided reality of who is more likely to get welfare. Every television news story on welfare reform showed footage of Black and Brown women with multiple kids hanging on them. Hardly ever did the news stories on welfare reform show that White people were also on welfare. Yes, per-capita there are a lot of Blacks and people of color on welfare. That's due to a lack of proper education and opportunities. But as far as straight-up totals of people on welfare? White people almost out-number African Americans, Hispanics, Asians and Native Americans combined in receiving welfare food stamps. For those of you who need to see proof, see below the Supplemental Nutrient Assistance Program, or SNAP chart. I show this only to give an example of how images and words have affected how negative many people of color are perceived to be, for doing the same thing as many Whites.

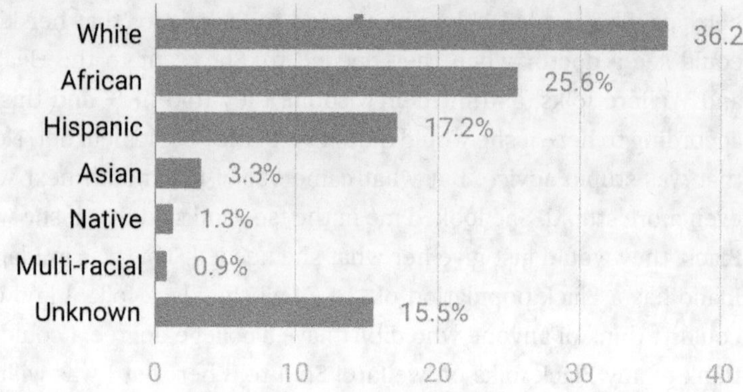

United States Department of Agriculture, 2016

Most Americans can't grasp this truth because the word welfare has become synonymous with Black people or other people of color. The truth of the matter is I'm sad that anyone has to be on welfare. But my point is that the American media and individuals have used many words to destroy the image of many of its people. Once those words and images are in our head, we become part of the ongoing problem of putting people from a certain group, religion or race in a easily describable, bowl, in which it doesn't take much thinking to access them. The only way we can get ourselves out of this type of mindless thinking is to learn to think for ourselves. There are many impartial sources of information at our disposal. They aren't as well-known as those sources that have an agenda of control, but they are out there.

The point I'm trying to make is what we say, the words we use and the images we show affects not only the people they're directed at, those very words and images also affect how we and our children view the world. Hopefully, what I've written sparks you to be careful of whom you listen to. Get to a mental place where you question what you think you know. Sadly, there's a reason why very young kids of all races, point to the dark brown baby doll as ugly and mean, when they themselves have never seen any such mean actions from people of color. However, our kids and young people do hear every negative word we say and every distorted image we show them. Then, we curiously wonder why our children grow up thinking that every immigrant is a terrorist, that all poor people are lazy or deciding to call a rose a toilet. If you're a Bible Believer, what was one of the first powers God gave Adam? Adam was given the power to name all of the animals, giving him dominion over them. Well, except for that silver-tongued serpent.

Racism in Church

The most racist day of the week in America is Sunday. People divide themselves by skin color and go to church to supposedly worship the same God. They do this, even though history and geography tell us that Jesus wasn't a blond hair blue eyed person. Most people living in the areas where Jesus lived, even today, have dark skin and hair of wool. Yet, American Christians have been taught that Jesus was White. This depiction is designed to make anyone who isn't white, feel inferior. How can a person of color feel superior knowing that the Son of Man is White? I used to travel the back roads of Idaho speaking about racism and God's love, at small churches. I can't tell you how many well-meaning White Christians came up and told me how Jesus also loved me. They would say it as if the information had been hidden from me. Sometimes I could see the pastor roll his eyes, because he knew, I knew. This person's White Christian superiority was flashing. It became apparent, that even in the realm of Christianity I was a second class. But, I was loved like a distant cousin, in the family of Christ. In my opinion, racism continues in the churches of America because many people in the church don't read information outside of the Bible. The church in America lives by the letter of the Bible and not by the spirit. Churches in America are too busy encouraging obedience from their congregations and not encouraging their congregations to seek the love of God. They sit in the huddle (church service) hearing about God's plan, but never break the huddle to run God's plan. They wait to be told what to think and what to do. Racism in churches stem from believing in the God of America, rather than believing in the loving God of the Bible. This causes Christians to interpret passages only in terms of how the passage fits the limits of their loves. Therefore, their interpretations are oftentimes incorrect. I'm adding two essays about racism in the church. I'm doing so because I believe when real love, from real lovers of Christ prevails, our country will become a better place to live. Racism needs Christians to come out of the church (huddle) and run the play (God's plan). And, because so many church people like Bible verses, I put some in the following article to let you know what I write comes from what has been written; not what I think. Do not be surprised if what is written in the Bible, contradicts what you think you know.

Essay #5. Do We Really Know The Bible and Its People?

The Bible has often been misinterpreted by those wanting power over others. All over this country Christians are behaving badly. Does the Bible talk about Christians with racist attitudes?

The Harper Study Bible Revised Standard Version, Numbers 12:1 says, "Miriam and Aaron spoke against Moses because of the Cushite woman whom he had married, for he had married a Cushite woman." The passage seems to be straightforward, until it's compared to the same passage from the King James Version, which uses the word Ethiopian instead of Cushite. Unaware Christians don't know that a Cushite is the same as an Ethiopian. Why would The Harpers Study Bible, copyrighted in 1952 (Old Testament) and 1946 & 1971 (New Testament), insert Cushite instead of just saying Ethiopian like most versions of the Bible? They didn't stop there, in the small print at the bottom of the page it says that Cushite and Ethiopian are generally considered to be the same, but that doesn't mean Moses' wife was Negress. They're suggesting there wasn't anything different about her skin color. Jeremiah 13:23 asks, "Can an Ethiopian change his skin or a leopard his spots?" This strongly suggests an Ethiopian's skin was different. Some scholars claim the word "Ethiopia "comes from the Greek word "Aithiopia" which is a combination of two words aitho- "I burn" and ops- "face", which would give us darkened or burned face people. God struck Miriam with leprosy for probably two reasons. First, Miriam shouldn't have gone against God's chosen leader. Second, like my Mama tells me, "God don't like people actin' ugly."

Even from the beginning of the Bible skin color didn't seem to be a problem. People of color fought against biblical heroes and some of them were biblical heroes. According to Wikipedia and many other encyclopedias, the origin of the word "Cush" is from the ancient Egyptian language and denotes a person of dark-skinned complexion. Cush was the eldest son of Ham and the father of Nimrod, who was the first mighty man and mighty hunter (Genesis 10:7). I Acts 8:26-40, it talks about Philip meeting and teaching an Ethiopian eunuch, sitting in his chariot reading, about Jesus.

Can some of what we think we know about Christianity be incorrect? Could it cause an attitude of superiority? In a 1939 article entitled "Ethiopian and the Origin of Civilization", written by John G. Jackson, he quotes French historian Constantin-Francois de Chasseboeuf Count de Volney. Count C. Volney wrote the following before he died April 25, 1820, "Those piles of ruins which you see in that narrow valley watered by the Nile, are the remains of opulent cities, the pride of the ancient kingdom of Ethiopia. ... There a people, now forgotten, discovered while others were yet barbarians, the elements of the arts and sciences. A race of men now rejected from society for their sable skin and frizzled hair, founded on the study of the laws of nature, those civil and religious systems which still govern the universe." A lot of what happened in the Bible took place in or near Africa, the cradle of civilization, therefore some of the people in the Bible, would have had to been people of color or even Black. American White Christians have all but eliminated people of color from the people of the Bible. One of the most hideous aspects of racism is when the dominant group wipes away the history and existence of the people they feel they must dominate. Normally the dominated people don't have the same color skin as the people doing the dominating. That's racism at its worst. Maybe this is the reason we hardly ever hear the following passage preached in churches. "If a man says he loves God but hate his brother, he is a liar; for he that love not his brother whom he hath seen, how can he love God whom he hath not seen" (1 John 4:20). Like my Mama says, "God don't like people actin' ugly."

Essay #6. The Color of God's Children

Every evening the nightly news tells America about another major concern. Our politicians are constantly, in their not so secret language, telling Americans how the demographics of America is changing. This is designed to add fear to the lives of people who think people of color are going to steal what rightfully belongs to White people. One of the biggest group of people who live in this fear, are people in the church. Just for the record, this country is more than the demographics of the people who live in it. If we did America correctly, we would feel a spirit of togetherness. Instead, people outside the church, look at people in the church and see no love. It is said that more people in America believe in God, than those who don't. So, if our country is mostly made up of people who believe in God, why aren't we a country showing each other the love of God? It can't be because we don't know the will of God is for us to love our neighbor as we love ourselves. If you have been a Christian for more than twenty minutes you should know and recognize Chapter 5 of Matthew, 'The Sermon on the Mount'. It tells us to be peacemakers and that we should hunger for righteousness and we're not to hide our light under bushel. So, if it isn't because we don't understand the love and the will of God, what's the problem? Could it be that we don't truly understand the importance of love? Could it be, because of our lack of understanding God's true love for us and the love He demands we have for each other, we have become more apathetic than apologetic? Are people in church starting to look like people in hate groups?

Do you realize that every unjust, violent, hateful and greedy situation perpetrated in this country ultimately starts with the lack of love and caring? Deep beneath the soil within the roots of the evil doers, there is a search for their promise of riches. We wrongly claim that money is the root of all evil. That's not what the Bible says. The Bible states in 1 Timothy 6:10, "For the love of money is the root of all evil; which while some coveted after, they have erred from the faith, and pierced themselves through with many sorrows." Here's an example how deadly the love of money can be. Many people think that the color of a man's skin in this country caused slavery and separation. The root of slavery in this country was about the greed for money. American's skin color hatred was invented later to justify the evils perpetrated by those who loved money more than people. In fact, many Christians partook and benefited in America's slavery systems. They too justified it by declaring Africans less than human. Today this same love of money continues to cause a human skin color separation. Notice that I didn't used the word "race". That's because I believe there is only one "race". It's called the "Human Race", made by God.

In Genesis 4:9 God asks Cain about the whereabouts of his brother Abel. Cain answers, "Am I my brother's keeper?" The answer to that age-old question is, who is my brother? The answer is, we are all brothers and sisters in Christ. The following question deserves to be asked and answered. What is the number one problem in society today? Evangelist Billy Graham said in the Foreword of "Breaking-Down Walls" by Raleigh Washington and Glen Kehrein, "Few issues trouble our world as persistently as the conflict between different races and backgrounds." He goes on to say, "Of all people, Christians should be concerned about racial strife. And yet all too often, we must confess, we have been content to stand on the sidelines and let others take the lead in racial reconciliation. At times we have even been satisfied with the status quo." To be honest I trust very few White men, but I trusted Billy Graham. Over the years the man has proven that his walk and his talk live in the same body. That doesn't mean he is perfect. He has had to apologize for a stupid comment or two in his life. Just for the record, I don't trust very many Black, Yellow, Red or Brown men either.

Matthew 19:19 says, "Honour thy father and thy mother and thou shall love thy neighbor as thyself." When asked about which is the greatest commandment in the law Jesus answered in Matthew 22:39, "And the second (commandment) is like unto it. Thou shall love thy neighbor as thyself." So, why are so many Christians choosing to love only those who look like they look; talk like they talk and live in their neighborhoods?

Attending church, praying a lot, and at the same time doing very little about social problems in America, has become an American Christian ritual. The ritualistic expression of apathy works as an enemy to the work of Christ, and it's a springboard to allowing racism to exist. It is one of the main reasons why our society is in the shape it is in. Sadly, this Christian apathy causes a veil to drape over the true love of Christ; hiding us from a world torn apart. We need Him dearly. Shamefully, too much of this Christian apathy is being taught by preach-so-they'll-come-back-next week, type pastors and preachers. It's impossible for an apathetically filled Christian society to do the work Christ appointed us to do, which is to love. While racism isn't hate, it is perpetrated because of a lack of love. This lack of love makes racism a Christian and church issue!

The question must be asked: Can God Bless America? If we understood the true nature of God, this question becomes very interesting. God is the God of the universe. This makes God the Father of us all. So, we are all 'Children of God'. Did not our Father, God, send his Son to die for all His children? Aren't brown, yellow and black skinned people brought here as slaves, also children of God? Aren't the red skinned people who lived and hunted in this land, long before the Mayflower arrived, children of God? Aren't all the people with brown skin and yellow skin who were forced to work on the railroads, children of God? Don't you think the Father of all these people is upset that His children of color are not being treated equal by His White children? Don't you think God would be equally upset to see that His Christian family is just as hateful and uncaring as many of those who have not accepted His love? Therefore, I ask again, can God bless America?

Those old enough to remember the tragic events of September

11, 2001, remember how it left us all in shock. Remember how Americans pulled together? I also remember how shocked I was, regarding how quickly our racial attitudes got back to normal. Just for the record, the normal I'm talking about has never truly been right in America. The only people who have gained anything from this tragic event are the people who make American flags.

Christians in America have never shown the world the power of God's love. What would happen if Christians showed the world that they understood the mistakes we've made and are ready to correct them? What if Christians unify and become strong enough to help society rid this country of racism and hate? There's a song that says, "With God as our Father, brothers all are we. Let me walk with my brother in perfect harmony. Let peace begin with me. Let this be the moment now. With every breath I take. Let this be my solemn vow. To take each moment and live each moment in peace eternally, let there be peace on earth and let it begin with me." Taking this one action will make this country a stronger place for everyone regardless of skin color.

God must be sick and tired of the church praying for answers He has already given. When will the church do love, rather than just pray about it? When will the church learn to reconcile with people and instead of condemning people? When will the church learn that empathy creates compassion and compassion creates love? When will the church learn love changes people? Love is a tool which can help make America the land of milk, honey and equality.

The other night on television I watched as hateful people taught their children to hate people of color and Jews. At the same time, they worshiped God. Can the One True God bless that? 1 John 4: 20-21 says, "If any man say, I love God and hate his brother, he is a liar: for he that loves not his brother whom he has seen, how can he love God whom he has not seen? And this commandment have we from Him, that he who loves God love his brother also."

A true follower of God or a true patriot cannot be a racist person. Just as a person who follows God's word is different than someone who just prays, so is the difference between a racist, a non-racist and an anti-racist.

Racism in Elementary, Middle and High School Education

According to World Population Review, the United States is the most powerful country in the world. According to USA Today of the top 25 richest countries in the world, the United States is ranked 11th. Yet, as far as education for the people of the most powerful and one of the richest countries in the world, the World Top 20 Project's International Education Database 2018 ranks the United States 26 out of the 201 countries with the following countries not being ranked: England, Northern Ireland, Scotland, Wales, Monaco, Vatican City, Mayotte (France), Reunion (France), Canary Islands (Spain), Madeira (Portugal), Melilla (Spain), Saint Helena (United Kingdom). This means the United States isn't doing a great job overall, when it comes to education its people. Yet, one of this country's most insidious forms of racism is not providing people of color the same level of education as it does whites. Here's why not being well educated causes generational poverty. While more money seems like the most obvious way out of the poverty cycle, it is becoming more and more obvious that having money must be accompanied by having an education. If money is not accompanied by education, the uneducated individual or group of people will eventually lose their monies and will not have continual access to more money, or the knowledge to grow their monies. A person can end up with a job paying a decent wage, but if they are uneducated, they will always be one paycheck from being homeless. While this is true for all races of people in this country, it is especially true for people of color. In my opinion, the system which is run by whites understands this and therefore under-educating people of color appears to be an ongoing and on-purpose process. I'm not talking about athletes or entertainers of color who make millions of dollars. But then again, a lot of those entertainers and athletes also end up broke. Why? Because while they're talented, many don't have the education to know what to do with their money. Many times, their wealth has little to no longevity. When their playing days or entertaining days are over, so is their ability to grow their money.

The evidence of racism in elementary, middle and high school education is best revealed with the graduation rate of most groups of students of color. Black and Hispanic students graduate at a lower rate than White and Asian students. I think this is partially due to the fact that eighty percent of teachers at the elementary, middle and high school levels are White. In many cases this creates a cultural communication gap, since the student of color population in America's school system is now over 40%!

It is no longer enough that beginning teachers leave college with the experience and education for teaching White middle income students. As with our nation, the faces in the classroom have increasingly more colors and cultures. In order to teach all students, teachers must be able to communicate with all students.

Research shows that the communication process used by a significant number of classroom teachers is a superior-subordinate type of communication. It is basically a model of communication known as linear. In their linear model, there is a sender (encoder) and receiver (decoder), channel, message and noise (Adler & Rodman, p. 11, 1997). In the linear model one person speaks and dominates the conversation. The persons speaking, (White teachers), are always in total control. In conversations between African Americans, the conversational lead changes throughout the dialogue. This exchange of dialogue from students of color is in line with a model of communication known as transactional. This model indicates that as communicators we are simultaneously sending and receiving messages (Adler & Rodman, p. 15, 1997). Students of color tend to both send and receive messages while in the process of communicating. In the classroom teachers perceive this style of communication as assertive and aggressive. Research suggests that

Whites and people of color communicate differently. For instance, African Americans generally communicate more assertively than European Americans (Orbe & Harris, 2001; Ribeau, Baldwin, & Hecht, 1994, p. 100).

In the classroom, communication breakdown often occurs when students do not understand the language or meaning of the teacher's message. Breakdown can occur also when the teacher doesn't understand the language or meaning of the student's message. When cultural and socio-economical barriers are added to the communication process, miscommunication is likely to occur. A majority of teachers are not aware of barriers affecting communication and the teaching process, making it difficult to relate to, inspire or even effectively communicate with students of color. The outcome of miscommunication and ineffective communication between teachers and students of color is predictable. Not preparing teachers to deal with ineffective communication with students of color is a form of racism.

Leadership, from the school district level, must raise awareness of teachers and prepare them to deal with multiculturalism within their classrooms. There is a need for new strategies in teacher recruitment and better preparation of our current recruits for working with diverse populations (Cockrell, Placier, Cockrell & Middleton, 1999, p. 351). The leadership of our educational system must decide to institute steps to solve miscommunication and in-effective communication. America's educational system must deal with this lack of multicultural training, before teachers reach their multi-cultured classes. Teachers must be educated and in many cases re-educated to understand students from various racial, ethnic, and cultural backgrounds.

Another difficulty that affects communication between students of color and White teachers is the attitude by teachers, "I don't see color. All I see are students." I've spoken to many White teachers who have proclaimed to have this attitude of "color blindness". Such an attitude makes solving the communication differences impossible. "My own experience with White teachers, both preservice and veteran, indicates that many are uncomfortable acknowledging any student differences and particularly racial differences. Thus some teachers make such statements as "I don't really see color, I just see children" or I don't care if they're red, green, or polka dot, I just treat them all like children" (Ladson-Billings, 1994, p. 31). White teachers must acknowledge the uniqueness that students from different cultures can bring to the classroom. Foremost they must be willing to accept the fact that these students are present in their classrooms. "This is not to suggest that these teachers are racist in the conventional sense. They do not consciously deprive or punish African American children on the basis of their race, but at the same time they are not unconscious of the ways in which some children are privileged and others are disadvantaged in the classroom. Their "'dysconsciousness' comes into play when they fail to challenge the status quo, when they accept the given as the inevitable" (Ladson-Billings, 1994, p. 32).

Since education more often than not, leads to discovering ways of earning a living, starting a business and finding one's way to happiness, not having an education limits one's opportunities. Black students and students of color must have teachers who understand their ways of thinking and communicating, in order to receive the same education as their White counterparts. As of today, America's school system is not putting much effort in leveling the learning field.

Essay #7. Education is Still The Best Bet For Defeating Racism and Poverty

I write this piece at the risk of sounding repetitive. It's too important of a problem, especially in today's version of America, to not keep on the forefront of peoples' mind. To rule a people, it is generally thought that you must control how they think. You must control what they think. Last, but not least, you must control their ability to evolve in their thinking.

AN ACT TO PREVENT ALL PERSONS FROM TEACHING SLAVES TO READ OR WRITE, THE USE OF FIGURES EXCEPTED

Whereas the teaching of slaves to read and write, has a tendency to excite dis-satisfaction in their minds, and to produce insurrection and rebellion, to the manifest injury of the citizens of this State: Therefore, Be it enacted by the General Assembly of the State of North Carolina, and it is hereby enacted by the authority of the same, That any free person, who shall hereafter teach, or attempt to teach, any slave within the State to read or write, the use of figures excepted, or shall give or sell to such slave or slaves any books or pamphlets, shall be liable to indictment in any court of record in this State having jurisdiction thereof, and upon conviction, shall, at the discretion of the court, if a white man or woman, be fined not less than one hundred dollars, nor more than two hundred dollars, or imprisoned; and if a free person of color, shall be fined, imprisoned, or whipped, at the discretion of the court, not exceeding thirty nine lashes, nor less than twenty lashes. Source: "Act Passed by the General Assembly of the State of North Carolina at the Session of 1830–1831" (Raleigh: 1831). From Wikipedia.

A website titled "Fight Municipal Court Abuse (court.rchp.com) includes the following in its list of significant anti-black laws:

- 1819, Missouri: Prohibited assembling or teaching slaves to read or write
- 1829, Georgia: Prohibited teaching blacks to read, punished by fine and imprisonment
- 1832, Alabama and Virginia: Prohibited whites from teaching blacks to read or write, punished by fines and floggings
- 1833, Georgia: Prohibited blacks from working in reading or writing jobs (via an employment law), and prohibited teaching blacks, punished by fines and whippings (via an anti-literacy law)
- 1847, Missouri: Prohibited teaching blacks to read or write

The last of these was only 171 years ago. Many other states passed similar anti-literacy laws; some with even stricter punishments. Think about the mindset put into place to make such educational control happen. There's no way those legislative and attitudinal policies go away overnight. While not all states adopted such laws, many did. So, what does old anti-literacy laws have to do with people today? Today, the lack of an education effects all poor and disenfranchised people. However, I don't think I'd be stepping out on a limb by saying education is especially important to people of color in general and Black people in particular.

As someone who has worked with low income students for over 22 years, it saddens me when I see students who don't take their education seriously. What makes me angry is seeing this country downplay the importance of educating the poor and those stuck in generational poverty. Think about it, of all the things slave owners could do and did, to their slaves, why was keeping them uneducated so important? There's something called Sapir-Whorf Hypothesis, which basically says that our language, thoughts and the words we use, shape how we view our environment and the world we live in. Therefore, if someone, or if a group or institution, can control how you're educated, they can then have the ability to control what you think.

So, if a group of people remain uneducated, then they will be at the mercy of the rich and powerful. Sooner or later the rich and powerful will realize that it is to their benefit that not only should people of color be uneducated, but everyone who isn't rich and powerful, should be un-educated. Recently, I asked a classroom full of high school students, who happen to be Mexican, most of them low income, how are they feeling about their future. They said that they were scared. I few days later, I asked a classroom of low-income White, high school students, the same question. They said that they were scared. How can a country that is supposed to be so advanced, create such fear in its young?

Apparently, there's no longer a need for anti-literacy laws. Produce fear in the young and they'll under-achieve. There's no fear of giving the talented athletes a ton of money, because a lot of them won't be educated enough to be a threat to the rich and the powerful. What would happen if Michael Jordan or Tiger Woods thought like Mohammad Ali or Colin Kaepernick and really gave a shit about racism and the poor? Give Kaepernick time and people will begin to accept him being mentioned in the same breath as Ali. They're linked today because they were punished for their beliefs. Ali was punished by the government, in the 60's. Kaepernick was punish by the American people, in 2016. Both were victims of racism. Some American people hid their racism by calling their dislike of Kaepernick, patriotism. But racism called by any other name is still racism.

Because of what I see going on in this country, from the White House to the outhouse (well actually the White House has become an outhouse, sorry I couldn't resist); I had to tell both groups of high school students, I too am scared. But I also told them that their greatest weapon is their ability to think. I told them, "If my knees didn't hurt so bad, I'd get down on them and I'd beg you not to allow anyone to steal your education away from you." I often told them, being uneducated (educated isn't always about having college degrees), makes a person feel that they have few choices. And the truth of the matter is, in general, uneducated people do have fewer choices. An education, most of the time, gives a person a way and an opportunity of seeing and exploring, oftentimes, seen and unseen choices and avenues.

Someone had on Facebook not too long ago, a picture of a Black person trying to climb a tree and another Black person is pulling him/her down. As Black people we must learn; if we aren't helping our young climb, we are aiding those who are pulling them down. And I don't mean sending them to basketball camps. In the same Facebook picture there was a White person climbing a tree and someone is actually trying to push him/her up the tree. I don't know how old the picture was, but I would update the picture by showing the new America, which would show the rich and powerful at the top of the tree, cutting off branches that say "education, freedom, future, peace of mind". What I'm trying to say is, we've reached the point where racism exist amongst those who have very little, because those who have a lot want it to. They want us to keep fighting amongst ourselves, while they take away our education and opportunities, which are our lifeline to a better way of life.

Chapter Three: 3rd Step To Becoming An Anti-Racist

NOTE: Here in chapter three on non-racist, I'm going to use a scenario as an example to show the actions of someone who is a non-racist. I will use the same scenario in chapter four, so the reader can compare each action. This scenario is based on a true situation. Of course, only one of the versions happened. Which version do you think actually?

3rd Step for becoming an anti-racist: **You must understand what a non-racist person is and work towards becoming an anti-racist.**

What is a non-racist?

A non-racist person does not use their race-based power to mistreat people based on their race or skin color. **A non-racist person** does not use his or her race-based powers to control and/ or destroy the lives of people who are not the same color he or she is. **A non-racist person** does not believe that their own race is superior to all other races. **A non-racist person**, while he or she does not believe the things a racist believes, non-racist people, **do very little** to positively change the negative race situation in their personal environment or in this country. Here's an example of why a non-racist must move to the next level and become anti-racist.

A non-racist act

Living as a Black man, there are racist things that happen that you never forget. This day was such a nice day. There should be a law. Racist things aren't allowed to happen on nice days. Well, regardless of the weather, I was about to add another racist situation to my life's collection. It was a little after five o'clock. Most people were trying their best to deal with five o'clock going home traffic. I stopped to pick up something at the drugstore. As I walked through the doors, I noticed that there weren't very many customers. I greeted the lady behind the counter. She didn't greet me back. I didn't think much of the fact she ignored me. Maybe she was having a bad day. I walked down the aisle to get what I came into the store to get. I smiled and said hello to a very pleasant White woman. She said hello back and smiled. I walked towards the counter to pay for my merchandise. The woman at the counter saw me and turned her back. I stood there waiting for her to come to the cash register. Meanwhile the pleasant looking White woman walked up and stood beside me. The lady behind the counter immediately addressed her. The pleasant woman gave the lady behind the counter a stern look. She paid for her merchandise and left. The lady behind the counter then helped me.

The pleasant White woman did nothing wrong. She gave the woman behind the counter a stern looking, letting her know that she knew what the woman behind the counter was doing. And like pleasant non-racists do, she paid for her goods and moved on. However, her kind of behavior during a situation like this does nothing to rid this country of racism. Read the chapter on anti-racist to find out about a better way pleasant woman could have dealt with the woman behind the counter.

Because the non-racist turns a deaf ear to today's overt racism, racism continues. Being non-racist is very dangerous in the fight against racism. The reason some non-racists do nothing to stop racist situations, is because deep down they have their own racist tendencies. Many times, non-racist people are only non-racist in the light of day. But behind the scenes, in the dark, they hide their normal racist tendencies. Racists may even pretend to be non-racist to further their own agendas. A racist person could pretend to be non-racist and own a professional ball team. If people of color are making racist people money, they'll smile to the Black players' faces, but will tear them down behind their backs. A president could be a racist, but pretend to be a non-racist, based on the words he or she uses. However, their actions will eventually show their racist tendencies. Does this sound like someone you know? I started this book in 2017. I said back then, believe me, things will get worse, regarding racism in America.

Here's another example of a non-racist mentality. If a person is being attacked in an alley, the non-violent person would walk by or away. Later the non-racist would tell others how horrible it is, that someone would attack someone else in such a way. The non-racist person might even talk about how they, as a productive member of society, would never do such a thing. However, just talking about how horrible the attack was, didn't help the person being attacked. By the same token, just saying how horrible a racist situation might have been, doesn't help the person being racially attacked.

Chapter Four: 4th Step to Becoming An Anti-Racist

NOTE: Here in chapter four on anti-racist, I'm going to use the same true scenario I used in chapter three as an example of showing the different actions taken by an anti-racist. Therefore, the ending of the scenario in this chapter will be different than the ending of the scenario in chapter three. Again, this scenario is based on a true situation. Of course, only one of the versions happened. After reading this second account, ask yourself, which version do you think happened?

4th Step to becoming an anti-racist: **You must understand the difference between the actions of a non-racist person and the actions of an anti-racist.**

What is an anti-racist?

An anti-racist person does not hate people based on their skin color or race. **An anti-racist person** does not use his or her race-based powers to control and/or destroy the lives of people who are not the same color he or she is. **An anti-racist person** does not believe that their own race is superior to all other races. **An anti-racist person** does not believe the hateful things a racist believes. Anti-racist people **take actions** to try to change a negative racist situation, in order to stop the racist situation.

Living as a Black man, there are racist things that happen that you never forget. This day was such a nice day. There should be a law. Racist things aren't allowed to happen on nice days. Well, regardless of the weather, I was about to add another racist situation to my life's collection. It was a little after five o'clock. Most people were trying their best to deal with five o'clock going home traffic. I stopped to pick up something at the drugstore. As I walked through the doors, I noticed that there weren't very many customers. I greeted the lady behind the counter. She didn't greet me back. I didn't think much of the fact she ignored me. Maybe she was having a bad day. I walked down the aisle to get what I came into the store to get. I smiled and said hello to a very pleasant White woman. She said hello back and smiled. I walked towards the counter to pay for my merchandise. The woman at the counter saw me and turned her back. I stood there waiting for her to come to the cash register. Meanwhile the pleasant looking White woman walked up and stood beside me. The lady behind the counter immediately addressed her. The pleasant looking White woman gave the lady behind the counter a stern look. Then to my surprise she looked the woman behind the counter straight in the face and said, "He was here first."

The actions the pleasant woman took put a stop to that racist situation. This is the type of action needed to help stop racism. One of the main reasons racism continues in this country today, has more to do with the lack of action by non-racists, than it does with the actions of racists. There are more people who claim to be non-racist than there are people who claim to be racists. However, in order to rid this country of racism, we need the actions of anti-racists. To rid this country of racism faster, we need more people to move from non-racists to anti-racists. The movement for an equality-based society must include anti-racists who are willing to discover their battle zones and fight with all their might. Non-racists sympathizers, their well-meaning feelings, and their no actions, do nothing to help eliminate racism. While it is better for society that a person is non-racist than racist, it takes the actions of anti-racists to make positive change. Give the fight against racism your time, your talents and your money. Whatever you give, make sure it is more than your feelings. As I have said several times before, racism was done on purpose. Therefore, racism must be undone on purpose. So, which are you and what will you do?

What is An Anti-Racist?

An anti-racist person does not hate people based on their skin color or race. **An anti-racist person** does not use his or her race-based powers to control and/or destroy the lives of people who are not the same color he or she is. **An anti-racist person** does not believe that their own race is superior to all other races. **An anti-racist person** does not believe the hateful things a racist believes. Anti-racist people **take actions** to try to change a negative racist situation, in order to stop the racist situation.

Living as a Black man, there are racist things that happen that you never forget. This day was such a nice day. There should be a law. Racist things aren't allowed to happen on nice days. Well, regardless of the weather, I was about to add another racist situation to my life's collection. It was a little after five o'clock. Most people were trying their best to deal with five o'clock going home traffic. I stopped to pick up something at the drugstore. As I walked through the doors, I noticed that there weren't very many customers. I greeted the lady behind the counter. She didn't greet me back. I didn't think much of the fact she ignored me. Maybe she was having a bad day. I walked down the aisle to get what I came into the store to get. I smiled and said hello to a very pleasant White woman. She said hello back and smiled. I walked towards the counter to pay for my merchandise. The woman at the counter saw me and turned her back. I stood there waiting for her to come to the cash register. Meanwhile the pleasant looking White woman walked up and stood beside me. The lady behind the counter immediately addressed her. The pleasant looking White woman gave the lady behind the counter a stern look. Then to my surprise she looked the woman behind the counter straight in the face and said, "He was here first."

The actions the pleasant woman took put a stop to that racist situation. This is the type of action needed to help stop racism. One of the main reasons racism continues in this country today, has more to do with the lack of action by non-racists, than it does with the actions of racists. There are more people who claim to be non-racist than there are people who claim to be racists. However, in order to rid this country of racism, we need the actions of anti-racists. To rid this country of racism faster, we need more people to move from non-racists to anti-racists. The movement for an equality-based society must include anti-racists who are willing to discover their battle zones and fight with all their might. Non-racists sympathizers, their well-meaning feelings, and their no actions, do nothing to help eliminate racism. While it is better for society that a person is non-racist than racist, it takes the actions of anti-racists to make positive change. Give the fight against racism your time, your talents and your money. Whatever you give, make sure it is more than your feelings. As I have said several times before, racism was done on purpose. Therefore, racism must be undone on purpose. So, which are you and what will you do?

10 Beliefs of An Anti-Racist

1. Recognize who you are and how your life experiences have colored the lens through which you view society. Be honest about who you are and what you think and believe.

Question: What do you think this means?

2. You must know what an anti-racist is.

Question: What do you think an anti-racist is? Racism was done on purpose and it must be un-done on purpose.

3. You must believe that all people are created equally. This includes doing more than just saying it. It includes living it.

Question: What do you think I mean when I say living it and not just saying it?

4. You must be brave and willing to be a social outcast.

Question: Why do you think being brave and willing to be an outcast is important?

5. You must be willing to think out of the box.

6. You must have knowledge of true history of how this country came to be. Knowledge is a tool. If history is wrong or distorted it becomes a weapon used by the group of people disseminating the wrong or distorted information about history.

Question: Why do you think this is so important to the people receiving wrong or

distorted information?

7. You must understand that racism cannot be perpetrated without power.

Question: Can you name the kinds of power it takes for racism to work?

8. You must understand the difference between covert racism and overt racism and the affects each has on the history of society.

9. Recognize people who talk the talk but do not walk the walk. These people would rather put up anti-racism posters on their walls

and drink coffee from mugs with anti-racism slogans written on them, than do the work of an anti-racist. (Use Rexall store woman example)

10. Don't think you need to take on the entire world. Use your anti-racism skills to conquer your own little worlds and then spiral outwards. Trying to conquer the entire world gets tiring and will burn you out.

Essay #8. Anti-Racism May Be An Answer

There's one thing about writing about racism today. There will never be a shortage of material. It seems there will always be someone, somewhere, who will eventually say something racist. Everyday people say racist things. Famous people say racist things. The difference is, the famous have more to lose than the rest of us–or do they? Because their racist rants oftentimes find their way into mainstream and social media, we find out about it sooner or later. The rest of us can say our racist comments in the privacy of our homes and among our friends. Remember when Hulk Hogan became the newest celebrity to add his name to the racist rant hall of fame? I liked the character Hulk Hogan. So, it saddened me to learn about his racist rant. If you remember, Hulk Hogan apparently got upset with his daughter after finding out she was dating a Black man. He then went on an "N" word rant, which was taped. The taping was 8 years prior but brought back to life and made public. From the news account, I remember listening to it and from a reporter who grew up loving Hulk Hogan, it was bad. The WWE (World Wrestling Entertainment) cut all ties with Hulk Hogan. I mean the WWE excommunicated him to the land of nonexistence. To his credit Hulk Hogan apologized profusely. But what else was he going to do?

Is the WWE's punishment going to undo, un-hurt or fix any problems in the Black community? Is the WWE's punishment going to help teach society not to say or do such racist things? The answer is no. Like I've said to you several times before, racism is an on-purpose act that must be undone, on-purpose. I think the WWE should have given Hulk Hogan a chance to undo his racist rant, by sending him to (in this case) a Black school or youth center and let him tell the kids and their parents why he's sorry for what he said. I think WWE and Hulk Hogan should have gone into their pockets and fix a problem in a poor Black school district. I think the WWE and Hulk Hogan should have started an after-school tutoring program to help Black kids do better in their school. This would have been an anti-racist act. This would have started the process of un-doing racism. If Hulk Hogan had made racist comments about Mexican people, Asian people, Native Indian people, or women, then what I'm talking about would apply to those communities. The same goes for any other race or group of people that have been offended by racist and hateful acts or comments perpetrated by wealthy people or organizations.

My point is, apologies aren't enough. With all the racist rants and acts that are going on in this country, nothing is being done to undo racism. Firing people who make racist, sexist or any other hateful comments, doesn't do anything for those communities or people hurt by the comments. An anti-racism approach needs to be taken. These communities need to demand more than apologies. Firing people who make racist comments does not educate or re-educate anyone. If society stays uneducated, racism will continue; Headline: "Racist person fired! End of Racism!"–probably not.

Chapter Five: Essays for Discussion- What is Racism? In A Nutshell

Sometimes it is difficult for White people to truly understand racism. The main reason is because they do not want to learn about this country's ugly past. They don't want to hear about slavery, Jim Crow, lynching or the civil rights movements. They certainly don't want to hear about how they are currently prospering from all the horrible things that happened to Black people and people of color in the past, or the things currently happening. Unfortunately, the problem is, until White people truly understand racism, they can do nothing to stop it. Therefore, racism will continue until the end of time. Just saying that gives me the creeps! However, I know it to be true. As you read my writings you will begin to understand why I put the power of stopping racism squarely on the shoulders of White people.

Racism in America started as a financial arrangement. Africans were merely property used to produce financial wealth for White people. Don't forget many people already had or understood the concept of indentured servitude. So, the idea of having someone else do your hard work was not a new concept. In America racism became an attitude, labeled and tagged by skin color. The African had the most distinguishable skin color. The Native Indians knew the land too well. It was difficult to capture and keep them. White indentured servants could escape to another town and mix in with all the other whites. The owners didn't have the technology to put out an all-points bulletin on a white male or female. There was no place for black-skinned people to hide. Often, if you were a breathing Black person, you belonged to someone. Escaping this was difficult to do. This made black-skinned people prime, permanent slavery prospects.

Slavery didn't have to become what it became, but like the old saying goes, absolute power corrupts absolutely. The greed for power and the corruption of power led to the demonization of Black people. To keep their slavery enterprises up and running the slave owners had to get into the heads of other whites. They did this by convincing whites that the slaves weren't completely human. This meant that Black slaves must be part animal. This mentally gave slave owners a psychological out, regarding the mistreatment of Black people. If Black people weren't humans, slave owners felt they could do anything they wish to them. However, classifying slaves as animals was an evil mind trick. One of the main reasons there are light-skinned Black people in this country has to do with White slave masters having sex with Black slave women. So, were the White slave masters purposely having sex with animals? No. The main reason for declaring Africans only part humans was to be able to count them and treat them as animals. The African male presented a different problem, even though some males were sexually assaulted. This was an act to belittle their manhood. The slave owners had to control him from the outside in. Other times, he was beaten to submission and then his mind was ready to be worked on. It was sort of the opposite of Jesus' way of teaching the five thousand. He fed their stomachs, in order to feed their souls. The slave owners beat the black male physically, so he could enslave and control him mentally.

The mental aspect of enslaving the Black man affected the White man. He began to truly believe that he was superior. He passed that superior attitude to his kids, generation after generation. After slavery was abolished and even until this day, the attitude of white superiority remains. My overall opinion from living amongst White people is that in general, they truly believe they are superior to anyone who isn't white, but this is especially true when it comes to Black people. As a Black man, to understand this is the first step to understanding the true effects of racism. By understanding their superiority complex I can show most White people where they lost their identity, culture and heritage. Once they understand what they have lost, I can show them how they are still taking advantage of their whiteness. I can show them how by using their whiteness to their advantage, they are continuing to contribute to racism.

Don't get me wrong, I know many White people who do not have a racist bone in their bodies. Still, a lot of them unknowingly use their white superiority. I see it all the time when it comes to dealing with the poor and disadvantaged. In my own personal life, I'm able to use white folks' white superiority against them. Because I'm a big Black man, with a loud voice, they don't see me as someone who has an above average-education (doctorate level). In the field of education, I get talked down to almost every day of my life. I'll say this right now. Next to religion, education is one of the most racist institutions in America! After I earned my doctorate, I was having a conversation with a White guy I knew. He told me that I would probably not get a position at the university we worked at, because I went and got a degree that put me on the same level as the White men in the good ole boys club. They were already afraid of my experience but saw themselves better than me because my experience didn't equal up to their education. At age fifty, I got the education (doctorate) to complement my experience. This White guy told me that with both experience and education I scare the White men at our university. To this day I have never held a position at this university, which would be considered commensurate to my education and experience level. This is one covert manner in which racism continues. The very people who consider themselves to be non-racists, do more harm than good because they need to move to the next level–anti-racist.

Ingredients of Racism

This writing comes from an academic perspective of racism rather than from the heart. I hope what I write sparks conversations. I don't expect everyone to like or agree with my words. I do know this: actions may speak louder than words, but knowledge is the foundation for corrective, positive action. A knowledgeable foundation is a positive tool for fighting against the tyranny of racism. To fight racism, we must know the ingredients within America's brand of racism. To fight racism, we must be willing to feel uncomfortable. To fight racism, we must understand that everyone and I mean everyone, will eventually be affected by the manifestations of racism.

The first and perhaps the main ingredient of racism is power. Racism doesn't work without power. If racist acts against a person or group of people **didn't have the power** to interfere with, control or destroy lives, families, and the ability to learn, discover and prosper; then a person or a group of people's racist attitudes would mean very little. If there were no power in racism, racist people would be like the grumpy old uncle, sitting in the corner, on Thanksgiving. The other relatives just tolerate him. However, in America, racism **does have power**. Racism has the power via television, newspapers, books and history, to define who a group of people are and then treat them accordingly. Racism also has the power to persuade people to believe and say; those who speak out against racism are un-American and un-patriotic. Racist do this by using that tired-ass statement," if you don't like how things are in America, then leave it".

The second ingredient of racism is a faulty education system. When people's education is faulty, those in power can convince them of anything. A faulty education has the potential to happen to more than just people of color. This is necessary because, there must be friendly fire casualties, whilst perpetrating racism on

America. So, there are well meaning people walking around with a faulty sense of superiority, because of a faulty education. Here are two examples of faulty education.

#1. Several years ago, I took a group of (majority of them White) students on a field trip to Pendleton, Oregon. We visited the community college there, but it was walking through the city underground, where Asian people had to live while they built the railroads, that taught the students the biggest lesson. Many of them were visibly shaken. Their history books never taught them about how Asians people were not allowed in town after dark.

#2. In a college course I was teaching in 2013, called 'Sociology of African Americans', I asked the students to get into groups with the students closest to them. Of the forty students, there were nine students of color. Five of (two Hispanics and three African Americans) ended up in the same group. After a couple minor in-class projects, I assigned the major project. At that point groups were given the choice, via voting, on whether to stay in their same groups or change groups. The group consisting of the 5 students of color, apparently not satisfied with their group's performance, voted not to stay in their group. The rest of the class (about 30 White students and 4 other students of color), voted to remain in their groups. Unfortunately for the group consisting of only students of color, this meant they had to stay in their group. Over a month later the major group projects were due. Two students from the group consisting of only students of color staged a protest. Without telling the other group members, they ignored the rules of the group project. They angrily addressed the class. According to them, they were at a disadvantage for having to do such an important group project, in a group consisting of only students of color. According to them the White students had an academic advantage. They call themselves "the disenfranchised". They called the White students "privileged". Here's the bottom line. Earlier, I'd learned that both college students (over 30 years of age) were educated in school systems with no teachers of color. They really believed being in a group of students of color made them academically inferior. By the way, the other students of color in the group didn't feel academically inferior. They'd come from more diverse teaching environments.

The third ingredient of racism is apathy. In the last writing I mentioned, racism was done on purpose and it must be un-done on purpose. Therefore, sitting around talking about how bad racism is, without instituting corrective, positive actions, only feeds racism. The group who makes me the saddest are Christians. Christians should be at the front of the line in ridding America of racism. As Christians we have the help of the number one playmaker of all time, but our fear of dealing with racism has put Him on the bench. We sit in our huddles (Churches) marveling at the plays He wrote for us. We never actually break the huddle and run His plays. Jesus told His Disciples to "Go". He wanted them to leave the room they were hiding in and go tell the world the good news. If prayer was all there was to helping man love and be reconciled to Him, Jesus would have told His Disciples to stay in the room and pray hard. However, Jesus knew prayer without action was not enough. Here are two Bible passages that really make me wonder about what being a Christian is about. Matthew 7:21-23, talks about what people expecting to enter the Kingdom of Heaven can expect. He tells those people that He never knew them, even though they did many wonders in His name. What people is He talking about? In 1 John 4:20 it says, "If someone says, "I love God," and hates his brother, he is a liar; for he who does not love his brother whom he has seen, how can he love God whom he has not seen?" These passages are rarely preached from the pulpit.

The fourth ingredient of racism is our "Melting Pot" mentality. America needs to rid itself of the "Melting Pot" mentality. It sounds good at first glance, but if looked at closely, the melting pot theory of America asks people to give-up who they are and assimilate. From my perspective this is the very definition of racism. We have the dominate group of people telling everyone else, that to be good Americans you must shed yourself of who you are and become like me. That was fine in the old "I wanna be like Mike" commercials, but, a group of people shouldn't have to melt themselves down and become someone else, in order to live peacefully in this country. There's a big difference between living by the laws and customs of America and having to give up one's identity as a human being. A healthier perspective for everyone, is what I call the "Big Salad" mentality. There's nothing healthier than a big salad. In a big salad the tomato is allowed to contribute to the salad and make it better, by staying a tomato. The same goes for the lettuce, white and green onions, cucumber, red and yellow peppers, black olives, brown mushrooms and so on. Every item (group of people) added to the big salad (America) makes the big salad (America) better. The items (groups of people) do not have to change themselves into someone else. Americans should see America as a "Big Salad" rather than a "Melting Pot".

Again, racism was done on purpose. It must be un-done on purpose. Let's all try to do something to un-do racism. Hold discussions at your homes and churches. Read the history of someone of a different skin color. Finally, stop saying, "I don't see color." Unless you're physically blind you do see color, just like you see poverty. It's okay to recognize color and poverty, learn from them and even celebrate cultural differences. The greatness of America comes from the assortment of people and ideas available within America. If we forget this valuable tool, we'll lose the real America.

Black men talking about race and White people

This piece is meant to inform. Anytime something is meant to truly inform, it also has the potential to anger some people. Please understand my goal isn't to anger anyone, but I'll no longer water down my thoughts in order to spare feelings. When I see people duplicating the salute of Nazis, it is time to take off the gloves and say what needs to be said. I'll start with myself. I have been a Black clown, advocating for a freedom that Whites will never give to my people or any other people of color. I've realized this for some time now. I've just been too afraid to call it what it is, racism. I also think I was afraid if I called it racism, which is exactly what it is, that it would make me appear to be just as racist as the people I'm speaking against. Well, as of this second, I don't give a damn if the racism I've learned, experienced, fight against and write about makes anyone feel that I'm a racist. The truth of the matter is, if you keep reading and truly think, you will surely determine I'm not a racist. If you allow your feelings to totally guide you, instead of knowledge, you might just see me as a racist. For those willing to open their minds, just think of what I'm saying, as a tablespoon of a very nasty tasting medicine. However, oftentimes very nasty tasting medicine really helps to heal your sickness. Knowledge, like medicine, must be allowed to get into your system so it can do what it is designed to do.

Recently, I had a very interesting and strong conversation with some buddies of mine. I have known these guys since college. Back then we were all athletes on scholarship. Long-since graduated from college, we now deal with everyday life and taking care of our families. So, this makes us those so-called, non-existent group of college educated, Black fathers, who love their families. We exchanged thoughts and experiences and I learned a lot from our three-hour conversation on race and White people in America. Guess what? No one hates White people! In fact, two of us taking part in this conversation are married to White women and we have half White kids. And we've both told our kids, being half White has never and will never get a biracial person any brownie points in life or with White people. By the way, those people who insist that a Black person married to someone who isn't Black, can't speak out against racism and discrimination perpetrated on Black people and other people of color, can kiss my black ass!

In that conversation we talked about when White people say to a Black person or person of color, "when I look at you, I don't see black or color." First, not for one second do most Black people and people of color believe that statement. In fact, most Black people and people of color, probably take that as an insult and think it's a stupid thing to say. Just for the record, most Black people and people of color who are out in society working their asses off trying to be successful, aren't doing it to be White or to be more accepted by White people. So, news flash White people, unless you're physically blind or color blind, how can you not see the color of someone's skin?

School teachers are notorious for saying "when I look at students, I don't see color". By not acknowledging a student's identity, those teachers don't see the student for who they are. Then when the student doesn't act the way the teachers think they should act, which is what teachers are more comfortable with, the student becomes a classroom behavior problem. Students of color do not mind teachers seeing their color. They just want teachers to see and respect them for who they are and not pre-judge them, because of their color. Students want you to know that their skin color doesn't make them any less capable than the skin color of White students. Whether or not White teachers want to believe it or not, it is more difficult for students of color to navigate through America's racist educational system when teachers have a predetermined image of who they are and what their potential is. And when teachers are in denial and fear talking truthfully about race, it doesn't help them to truly understand students of color.

Here's where I think it goes awry. I swear it's like some White people think people of color are aspiring to reach some bastardized form of whiteness. And by telling us that you don't see our color, we've somehow reached a whiteness that is comfortable for you. That is not the case! We are proud of our blackness. Black people want to be respected for our contributions and abilities. We don't want any special treatment. Think about this. What kind of country would we have if after the end of slavery White people would have truly said, acted and believed in true equality? We would be living in a country that 100% believed that "All men are created equally". Instead we have a society where one group of people have decided that anyone who doesn't look like them is the enemy. As some White people began to accrue wealth, they had to find a way to keep other White people from attaining some of their wealth. They didn't want to share. So, an enemy had to be created. So, today, to even the poorest and whitest of towns and cities and even states, the Black man and other people of color have become the reason why low income White people can't or haven't reached the American dream.

People should be allowed to be proud of the color of their skin, no matter what color it may be. But at the same time, we must remember that using skin color as a identifying label, was pretty much made up because of this country's fascination with racism. In reality, no one comes from Black Land, White Land or Brown land, etc. We all are decedents of people who come from various countries. In many countries people differ in skin color but are still countrymen. So, to be more exact, I'm proud of my African and Native lineage, but I am an American and full blown citizen of The United States. There should be no "but not equal", at the end of who I am.

One of the other things I realized from our conversation is that White Americans are angry, but they are angry at the wrong people. I mean, let's look at the truth. The statistics really say if a White person is robbed or assaulted, it will probably be by another White person. But when a group of people control the media, they can turn and twist the facts and have White people believing that Black people and other people of color are going to rob them and do them bodily harm. Another truth, numbers-wise: there are more White people on welfare and abusing the system, than any other group of people in America. However, the media televises people of color when it does news of welfare and welfare reform. The wealthy people who hoard 95% of the wealth of this country are 99.9% White. Therefore, people of color, especially Black people do not have what White people feel they deserve and aren't getting. Notice, I didn't say "think they deserve". That's because for White people it's all about how they "feel". Thinking has nothing to do with their understanding of the race situation in America.

The anger that so many White people are feeling, isn't new to Black people and other people of color. All I can say is welcome to the damn club! However, White people's anger makes them susceptible to believe anything someone given a platform tells them. And nine out of ten times, the person standing on the platform will tell them, their lives would be so much better if America could get rid of people of color. I've never heard someone stand on their platform and declare a war on the wealthy. You know, the people who really have the power to dictate what goes on in the lives of White people.

Our conversation continued as we talked about the myth of Black on Black crime, in relationship to White on White crime and White on "everyone else" crime. For instance: There have been several policemen killed in the past few weeks by White killers, but the media isn't reporting it. They certainly aren't reporting it with the same vigor as they did when Policemen were killing Blacks or when a Black person killed a policeman. Mass shootings in this country have been white on white crimes, but they are never called white on white crimes. Can you imagine what the evening news would sound like if newscasters had to say, "There has been another white on white shooting" every time there was a white on white shooting?

Because white people own the media, there's absolutely no chance of that ever happening.

Three hours later our conversation ended. We hadn't solved anything outside the four walls of my friend's house. Yet, there was an internal peace in knowing I wasn't alone in my observations. I got into my car and drove home. The peace I felt didn't stop the thoughts I had on racism, racing through my mind.

Black Superheroes, Black Directors and Race

I want to comment on actor Anthony Mackie's comment regarding a Black director directing "Black Panther". He made his comment some time ago to the Daily Beast, which read "I don't think it's important at all. As a director your job is to tell a story. You know, they didn't get a horse to direct Seabiscuit!" Some have tried to say that Mackie is comparing a Black director to a horse. In my opinion that would be a stretch, even in a world that made sense. However, we live in a politically correct society, which rarely makes sense and looks for racist, homophobic and sexist statements in every word, every celebrity, politician or sports star says. And to be honest, most of these people don't help the situation very much. It seems they are constantly putting their feet in their mouths. However, this topic is too serious to waste time on a remark that is small in stature when compared to racism, which appears to be one of Hollywood's important problems.

I love the fact that movie technology has caught up with the superpowers of comic book superheroes. As a young black child, I always wanted to open my comic book and see someone who looked like me. I wanted to see a Black superhero eliminating the evil Electro-Head destroying the city. When I grew older and had my own kids, I remember taking them to their first superhero movie, Spiderman. Superhero movies became our tradition. My wife couldn't care any less about them; so, most of the time it was me and my sons. My wife did go to one of the superhero movies with us and promptly fell asleep. As my sons grew older, they noticed there weren't any Black superheroes. We knew of "Black Panther" and hoped someday they would make a movie starring him. We were happy when "War Machine" suited up for Iron Man 2 and "Falcon" suited up for "Captain America: The Winter Soldier". When my oldest son (the movie buff), told me that "Black Panther" was going to be made into a movie we were happy and decided, even though they would be finishing up college in 2018 (when the movie was released), we'd get together and go see it. Okay, so now you know how into superhero movies my boys and I, are.

I wanted "Black Panther" to be on the same level as the other superhero movies. I wanted it to be good. When I say as "good", I mean it couldn't be anything like any of the "Fantastic 4" movies. The first two were directed by a Black director, named Tim Story. The third "Fantastic 4" movie was directed by a White director named Josh Trank. The third "Fantastic 4" movie was worse than the first two "Fantastic 4" movies. I think that goes to show that the director's skin color, in this case was irrelevant. Neither one of those directors had what it took to make those "Fantastic 4" movies able to stand up next to Iron Man, Superman, Batman, Captain America, Spiderman, The Avengers or the two Hulk movies. "The Hulk" was directed by an Asian man named Ang Lee and "The Incredible Hulk by a Frenchman named Louis Leterrier.

The most important thing was, whoever would direct "Black Panther" must understand what makes a superhero movie a good movie. There would have to be a great story, great action, a great twist in the plot and an interesting and somewhat diabolical villain. When it comes to "Black Panther", the villain should be a "Black Panther" superhero type villain. Using modern technology, this villain should be doing pretty much the same things as in the "Black Panther" comics. Black directors should have the opportunity to direct a superhero movie, not because the superhero is Black, but because they understand how to direct a superhero movie, no matter what color the superhero is. F. Gary did a great job directing "The Italian Job". It wasn't a black movie. It was a great heist movie. Which proved that a Black director could direct a movie that isn't a Black movie. In fact, most people didn't or don't know that the director of "The Italian Job" was Black. I didn't know until a year or two later. When I found out who the director was, I thought the movie was still a great heist movie. Eventually I ended up buying it, not because the director was Black, but because it was a movie I really liked.

Black directors should not be limited to only directing Black movies. Just like White, Brown, Red or Yellow directors should not be limited to directing movies about people with skin the same color as theirs. Don't get me wrong, I would like to see more quality Black movies in general. A lot of Black movies tend to socially set Black people back a few steps. Most of those movies are directed by Black directors who care more about money than they do about how their movie makes Black people look. That's their right. And guess what? I have a right to not go and see those types of movies, and I don't. The bottom line is this: sometimes a movie needs a director reflective of the culture the movie is portraying. Sometimes a movie just needs a director with vision, creativity and a desire to entertain their audience. It would be nice if we could trust Hollywood to know and understand the importance of knowing the difference. But because we live in a racist, money greedy society, there is no quick fix to movie racism, just like there is no quick fix to society's racism. Maybe we, like Hollywood need to learn to say to ourselves, when in doubt, just do what's right. The truth of the matter is, left to their own devices, people in power don't do what is right. They do what's profitable. So, if a Black superhero movie, directed by a Black director can make a good enough profit, we'll see more of them. If it doesn't, they will go the way of the western. You can take that to the bank.

Do We All Really Get to Be Americans?

I saw a post on Facebook that said we, people of color, should stop calling ourselves African Americans, Asian Americans, Mexican Americans, Native Americans and so-forth. The post said that we should just call ourselves Americans. I don't think it's about people of color not seeing ourselves as American. I think it's more like us feeling like we're not being treated equally, as Americans. Not being treated as a full American, by those who consider themselves as the only Americans. This act causes the racial separation in this country, more-so than what we call ourselves. This perspective seems to lay the blame for America's racial separation square on the shoulders of people of color. If calling ourselves an American instead of African American, Asian Americans, Mexican Americans, Native Americans would get us all the benefits of being Americans, I think we'd do it in a New York second. This issue runs deeper than what people of color decide to call ourselves. Most people can't understand that the level of bigotry, hate, homophobia, plus all the "isms" we employ in America, has reached a new and dangerous height, even for America.

White European Americans better start paying attention. If you aren't wealthy, you have just been given a free membership to the club people of color have been members of for generations. A new thought has become apparent. The so-called real Americans believe you're an American only if you have real money. Even though the caste-system train has gained steam and has pulled away from the station, it doesn't mean that racism is something of the past. The caste system picks up where color skin stops. This allows the caste system to concentrate on its most important color, green. If you have a lot of green, you're in. It doesn't matter how much experience you have. It doesn't matter how intelligent you are. What matters is, who you are able to buy?

Look at this country's current presidential cabinet. It is the wealthiest cabinet in the history of this country. If any of the people given their positions, had to apply for their positions, on an even playing field with real applicants with just average position experience, almost every single one of the new cabinet members wouldn't make it through the first round of interviews. I am more qualified to be Secretary of Education for the United States, than the person who just got the job. I'm being serious. I have a doctorate in education leadership. I have taught in public schools for over twenty years. I taught at public universities for over fifteen years. My dissertation was about teacher communication with students from diverse backgrounds. And I certainly understand the proficiency versus growth debate. The new Secretary of Education for the United States is just wealthy and has never spent a day of her life learning in the educational system, let alone teaching in it. (Note: While I am more qualified than she is, I'm not qualified to be the Secretary of Education for the United States, but my point is: neither is she)

The new racism isn't about the overt physical manifestation of hatred. Yes, those who wish to do bodily harm to people of color still exist, but they're like the plantation policy holders from the days of slavery. Those plantation policy holders became what we today call police. Just like those plantation policy holders from the days of slavery, their job is to scare the slaves and keep them in check. Incidentally, those plantation policy holders, didn't sit at the masters' tables either. Today's hate groups don't get to sit at the table of today's wealthy. They sit at the feet of the wealthy waiting for the discarded scraps; it's their payment for keeping the public's focus on the overt racism. Meanwhile big money corporations perpetrate covert racism using money and power. The new racism is no longer relegated only to skin color and ethnicity. White hate groups of today are no more wanted by wealthy White society, than Black people and other people of color.

The situation with the Dakota pipeline access is a recent example of the game of money and power. Unless the Standing Rock Sioux and the other protesters can come up with a way to invade the deep pockets of Energy Transfer Partners or convince the people of North Dakota of the danger the pipeline would be to everyone if built, their movement is in big trouble with this new wealthy administration. Following the money trail has jumped to a new level, because greed has reached a new level. And, only a selected few in this country have the money and power to play this new game at this new level.

Would calling themselves Americans instead of Native Americans get them all the benefits the Energy Transfer Partners are getting from the new wealthy cabinet and administration? Probably not. Therefore, African Americans, Asian Americans, Mexican Americans and Native Americans shall we be.

Don't Shoot the Messenger

WARNING: If you rather accept things blindly, don't read this essay.

Those of you who have read my articles know that I feel the attack on the police officers in Dallas and Baton Rouge were cowardly. You also know that I feel the killing of unarmed Black men is also cowardly. However, the last shooting takes the cake. And luckily there is video footage to verify what happened. According to a story written by the Associated Press Wednesday, and the accompanying video, a Black therapist in North Miami who was trying to calm an autistic patient in the middle of the street says he was shot by police even though he had his hands in the air and repeatedly told them that no one was armed. The moments before and after the shooting were recorded on cell phone video and released to local media. The video shows Charles Kinsey lying on the ground with his arms raised, talking to his patient and police throughout the standoff with officers, who appeared to have them surrounded. "As long as I've got my hands up, they're not going to shoot me. This is what I'm thinking. They're not going to shoot me," he told WSVN-TV from his hospital bed, where he was recovering from a gunshot wound to his leg. "Wow, was I wrong." The shooting victim, from his hospital bed said that he asked the policeman, "Why did you shoot me?" He said the policeman replied, "I don't know."

But before I get into what I'm going to say, I believe eventually this recent shooting will give anti-violence groups and "Black Lives Matter" their smoking gun. There's no way the "All Lives Matter" movement can blame the victim for being shot. He was truly a therapist. The young man he was helping was really an autistic patient. The shooting victim had his hands up, while lying on the ground, on his back. For whatever reason the police had him surrounded, with their guns pointed at him. For what appears to be no reason at all, the police shot the man while his hands were up in the air. Luckily, they only shot him in the leg. Again, there's no blaming the victim. This guy was no threat to the safety of the policemen. Yet, they still shot him!

So, my question to you is, why is the shooting and killing of unarmed Black men happening? As wrong as these reasons are, revenge and retaliation are the reasons policemen are suddenly getting shot. I say suddenly and I will back up using that word in a second.

The problem with most people in America is that they are victims and they don't even know it. Often, those who are unaware that they are victims do a fair amount of damage. Sometimes when that damage is done, it causes a ripple effect. That's when things get confused and all hell breaks loose. This is exactly what has happened with the shootings of unarmed Black men and now the shootings of policemen. Misinformation is the culprit that makes America act stupid. We're all full of misinformation. That's because we allow the television news to educate us. Back in the days of Walter Cronkite, or the Huntley and Brinkley Report, we could depend on the truth. Today news is entertainment, designed to get ratings, not truth. It has gotten to the point where we are addicted to this brand of entertainment and have come to dislike true facts. We want drama, not boring facts. Facts make us think and we don't wanna think. We wanna be told what to think. Television news has done what drug dealers do. They tease you with a little, until you're hooked. Then they jack the price up. The American public has sold its soul to drama. If someone attempts to enlighten us with truth, we'll shoot the messenger.

In an article dated December 9, 2014 Eva Decesare writes, *the latest data from the Bureau of Labor Statistics (BLS), recorded a preliminary total of 4,405 fatal work injuries in the US in 2013. The BLS compiled that data to make a chart of the top ten most dangerous jobs. Guess who's not in the top ten. That's right, policemen. A report put out at the beginning of the year by the National Law Enforcement Officers Memorial Fund, highlights that lack of danger by showing that 2013 has had the "Lowest Level of Law Enforcement Fatalities in Six Decades" and the fewest officers killed by firearms since 1887.*

Here's the list of the most dangerous occupations.

10. **Construction Laborers**
Total fatalities for 2013 (based on preliminary data): **215**
9. **Electrical Power-Line Installers and Repairers**
Total fatalities for 2013 (based on preliminary data): **27**
8. **Farmers, Ranchers, and other Agricultural Managers**
Total fatalities for 2013 (based on preliminary data): **220**
7. **Driver/Sales Workers and Truck Drivers**
Total fatalities for 2013 (based on preliminary data): **748**
6. **Mining Machine Operators**
Total fatalities for 2013 (based on preliminary data): **16**
5. **Refuse and Recyclable Material Collectors**
Total fatalities for 2013 (based on preliminary data): **33**
4. **Roofers**
Total fatalities for 2013 (based on preliminary data): **69**
3. **Aircraft Pilots and Flight Engineers**
Total fatalities for 2013 (based on preliminary data): **63**
2. **Fishers and Related Fishing Workers**
Total fatalities for 2013 (based on preliminary data): **27**
1. **Logging Workers**
Total fatalities for 2013 (based on preliminary data): **59**

I've read several reports on dangerous occupations and the closest to the top ten policemen rank is 14. Therefore, I'm not saying there's no danger in being a policeman. What I'm saying is that everyone, citizens and policemen alike have bought into the notion that every policeman has to worry about getting home every night. And in our society, this fear of getting home, has become the theme song and excuse for shooting unarmed Black men. Yes, I know there are almost twice as many White people who get shot by policemen, but there are ten times more White people in America. If you do the math, you will realize that being Black in America highly subjects you, even though Whites outnumber Blacks, to the possibility of being shot by a policeman.

The police are the victims because they are put out on the streets suspect of damn-near every citizen they meet. Citizens are victims, especially Black citizens, because any move we make could get us killed. As citizens we should respect the police. We shouldn't have to be afraid of the police. I remember the days you could flag down a policeman, when you were in trouble. The way things are going now, you'll end up on the ground cuffed. If you resist, you could end up being shot. That isn't "To Protect and Serve". And to be honest it is probably difficult to protect and serve people if you're unreasonably fearful for your life. That is why truthful information is important and shapes the way we think. It shapes our attitudes about how we go about our days and how effectively we communicate with one another.

For law enforcement the trend has been clearly downward in the last 40 years. Police work is getting progressively safer compared with historical averages: **The fact is: being a policeman is not one of the most dangerous jobs you can have**, according to statistics from the Bureau of Labor. In five years, 2008 to 2012, only one policeman was killed by a firearm in the line of duty in New York City. Police officers are many times more likely to commit suicide than to be killed by a criminal; nine NYC policemen attempted to take their own lives in 2012, alone. Eight succeeded. In 2013, eight NYPD officers attempted suicide, while six succeeded. 2013 had the fewest police deaths by firearms since 1887 nationwide.

The national figures vary widely from year to year. In 2014, police deaths in the line of duty, including heart attacks, spiked upward from 100 in 2013, to 126 in 2014. (The most recent numbers available)

From 1970 to 1980 police deaths averaged **231** per year.

1980 to 1989: police deaths averaged **190.7**.

1990 to 1999: police deaths averaged **161.5**.

2000 to 2009: police deaths averaged **165**.

2013 to 2014: police deaths averaged **113**.

So how many policemen are there? Nationally, in 2008, state and local law enforcement agencies employed more than 1.1 million persons on a full-time basis, including about 765,000 sworn personnel (defined as those with general arrest powers). Agencies also employed approximately 100,000 part-time employees, including 44,000 sworn officers.

In Boise, where I live, there has only been one policeman, Officer Mark Stall, killed in the line of duty, in the history of the Boise Police Department (1903). And even that's one too many! I know the Chief of Police is out in the community, trying to get to know the leadership of the people of color in Boise. That's a great step towards making Boise safe for everyone, citizens and policemen alike.

America needs to sit down and stop pointing fingers. We need serious discussion about misinformation and false perception. We need to discuss how misinformation and false perception has made both policemen and citizens victims. Shooting it out isn't gonna work. Old procedures need to be updated and changed with the times. I want with all of my heart to value good policemen. I also want policemen to know that I matter to my family and friends.

Get out of line; and this will happen to you too!

All over the internet, one can see videos of policemen shooting, killing or detaining Blacks and people of color. Not for one minute do I think all policemen act this way. So, what's going on? Below is an excerpt from Willie Lynch's speech to slave owners. To read the entire speech Google "The Willie Lynch Letter".

I HAVE A FOOL PROOF METHOD FOR CONTROLLING YOUR BLACK SLAVES. *I guarantee every one of you that, if installed correctly,* **IT WILL CONTROL THE SLAVES FOR AT LEAST 300 HUNDREDS YEARS.** *My method is simple. Any member of your family or your overseer can use it.* **I HAVE OUTLINED A NUMBER OF DIFFERENCES AMONG THE SLAVES; AND I TAKE THESE DIFFERENCES AND MAKE THEM BIGGER. I USE FEAR, DISTRUST AND ENVY FOR CONTROL PURPOSES.** *These methods have worked on my modest plantation in the West Indies and it will work throughout the South. Take this simple little list of differences and think about them. On top of my list is "AGE," but it's there only because it starts with an "a." The second is "COLOR" or shade. There is* **INTELLIGENCE, SIZE, SEX, SIZES OF PLANTATIONS, STATUS** *on* plantations, **ATTITUDE** *of owners, whether the slaves live in the valley, on a hill, East, West, North, South, have fine hair, coarse hair, or is tall or short. Now that you have a list of differences, I shall give you an outline of action, but before that, I shall assure you that* **DISTRUST IS STRONGER THAN TRUST AND ENVY STRONGER THAN ADULATION, RESPECT OR ADMIRATION.** *The Black slaves after receiving this indoctrination shall carry on and will become self-refueling and self-generating for* **HUNDREDS** *of years, maybe* **THOUSANDS.** *Don't forget, you must pitch the* **OLD** *black male vs. the* **YOUNG** *black male, and the* **YOUNG** *black male against the* **OLD**

black male. You must use the **DARK** *skin slaves vs. the* **LIGHT** *skin slaves, and the* **LIGHT** *skin slaves vs. the* **DARK** *skin slaves. You must use the* **FEMALE** *vs. the* **MALE**, *and the* **MALE** *vs. the* **FEMALE**. *You must also have white servants and overseers [who] distrust all Blacks. But it is* **NECESSARY THAT YOUR SLAVES TRUST AND DEPEND ON US. THEY MUST LOVE, RESPECT AND TRUST ONLY US.** *Gentlemen, these kits are your keys to control. Use them. Have your wives and children use them, never miss an opportunity.* **IF USED INTENSELY FOR ONE YEAR, THE SLAVES THEMSELVES WILL REMAIN PERPETUALLY DISTRUSTFUL.** *Thank you gentlemen."*

Some people claim that the "Willie Lynch Letter" isn't real. Whether or not it is real, in my opinion, even in today's so-called technically advanced society, the above strategy is in play. Whenever Black people and people of color; sometimes with the help of Whites who are true patriots, start advancing, racism and violence rears its ugly head. I believe this racist violence to be the modern-day version of the information in the "Willie Lynch Letter". In the letter it also talks about how slaves will turn on each other. Can you say Colin Kaepernick and the rest of the Black NFL Players? Anyway, that's another article.

Because Black people and other people see this violence all over the internet, it truly makes us scared for our young. With recent shooting of Justine Damond, a White Australian woman, this violence should scare and infuriate everyone, regardless of your skin color. I will say, had this country done something about these shootings years ago when Blacks and people of color were being shot and killed, Justine Damond might still be alive.

When will this country learn that people in power, people in control, start their violence with the powerless and the disenfranchised and move their way up the economical chain? The goal of the rich and powerful is to control EVERYONE who isn't rich and powerful! Even the hateful and racist people of our society are just tools used to do the dirty work of the rich and powerful.

If White Nationalists could get rid of every person of color in this country, they themselves will become the new target of the rich and powerful. Just look at countries with little to no people of color (Russia for example). They must create people to hate because they are all people with white skin. It reminds me of the "Blue eyes, brown eyes experiment" done in the 60's (Google it). In an all-white classroom in the south, a White teacher gave power to the students in her class who had blue eyes. Read how racist White parents got, even though there were no people if color involved.

The point is, sometimes things don't change much. Sometimes things are just put into a shinier package. The videos of the killings of people of color that are all over the internet serve as a warning and a reminder to people of color. Just like the blackballing of Colin Kaepernick is a warning and a reminder to the rest of the Black players in the NFL. Get out of line and this will happen to you too. Soon, this message will apply to EVERYONE who isn't rich and powerful!

Of course, all lives matter, but...

If this country was a country that cared and treated everyone with respect, there would be no need for "Black Lives Matter". And please don't tell me respect is earned. Respect should be given until someone proves they don't deserve it. And when someone doesn't deserve it, then disrespect them if you must, but don't lay that person's ignorance on a whole race, culture or group of people. "Black Lives Matter" is important because right now in this country Black people are being killed for things we shouldn't be killed for. For Black people this is real! For Black People this breaks our hearts. To be honest, Black people need to scream "Black Lives Matter" because we, ourselves, need to truly believe and understand that "Black Lives Matter". Self- hate is prevalent in the subconscious of Black people. However every time Black people try to bring the matter to the forefront of society, which could help us deal with the hatred aimed at us and the hatred implanted in us, people want to water it down by coming up with something like, "all lives matter". Only a heartless individual would not understand that all lives matter. Isn't that exactly what "Black Lives Matter" is basically trying to say–'Include' us in all lives matters? Stop killing us like we don't matter. Stop mistreating us like we don't matter. Man, if we can't be honest about the racism and hatred going on in this country, it'll never get fixed. If you don't know that Black people are treated badly in this country, then you're ignoring the problem on purpose.

I had lunch last weekend with a friend of mine, I've known since college. He happens to be a Native Indian. He's a lawyer who has argued in front of the United States Supreme Court. He was telling how important it is that we respect Mother Earth. He explained to me the Native perspective. I told him that I totally agreed with what he was saying, but I have no hope for it ever happening, because man can't even respect his fellow man. Think about this if man can't respect his fellow man, he ain't gonna give a shit about the ozone layer, trees, recycling or anything else. As a Black man, I'll start worry about recycling when I have don't have to worry about my Black teenaged sons being stop for a tail-light and end up dead. I know there are other groups of people being mistreated in this country and they should scream out too.

Black people have had a history of having to scream, "What about us?" We hold these truths to be self-evident, that all men are created equal. The truth of the matter is Black people had to have a special amendment added because those great words of The Constitution didn't include us. In fact, many of the men who wrote those great words went back to their plantations and slaves. In 2015, in America, and by virtue of being an American, Black people shouldn't have to scream "Black Lives Matter". But until this country changes how it treats Black people it needs to be said repeatedly, "Black Lives Matter".

The "Gap Tool"

From slavery of the poor, to the lack of income by those who won't admit they're poor, the "Gap Tool" has always been a weapon of mass destruction, detonated by evil extremists. The "Gap Tool" is recognized by many names, such as, the haves versus the have nots, powerless middle class versus the disenfranchised minorities. And the "Gap Tool's" sole purpose has always been to divide society. Once divided, society will start grasping for anyone who is willing to give them a reason why life is so bad, even if the reason is a lie. Whatever one might want to call it, "Gap Tool" conquers all within its sights. The "Gap Tool" goal is to stretch and divide society so far from each other that even when people try to correct it, it will never be the same. Every few years the "Gap Tool" must be brought out, in order for evil to gain ground. It's a page from the Willie Lynch, school of obedient slaves. Doing horrible and vile things to the point where the victims accept any amount of release from the act. In fact, they will teach their children to obey the victimizer. Like me worrying so much about the lives of my sons, that I feel I must teach them to over-obey the police. I'm not talking about the normal respect good policemen deserve. I'm talking about having to obey to the point of feeling like the police are our masters, rather than civil servants who are paid via my taxes. That's the "Gap Tool" at work.

Everyone, but especially Black people need to wake up. Whenever you hear someone say "Let's make America great again", know you're hearing a code-phrase. Hatred has come like a thief in the night. It isn't wearing horns or wagging a tail. In this age, hatred dresses up in suits and ties. Hatred wears designer heels and power outfits. Hatred is educated enough to know that its old language will no longer work. In fact, hatred stands in the gap of ever flowing troubles of society to widen the distance of peace and harmony. The strategy works on everything from racial strife to political party separation.

The "Gap Tool's" dispenser's job is to confuse those who feel that they have somehow been cheated out of what should be solely theirs. To them, civil rights, women's rights, gay rights and even basic human rights, are all wrong. They just want America to go back to being great again.

Let's just examine at what point and time America was so great that we should all want to go back to it. And who was America great for at that time? Let's see, do Black people who want to go back to the time of slavery, or Jim Crow, lynching, and even worse police brutality? Do women want to go back to not having the vote, go back to when there were no laws for being beaten by their boyfriends or husbands; or the good old, unequal pay for the same job, dynasty? Would Native people want to go back to reliving the breaking of every treaty made with them? Then again, Native people may want to go back before the Mayflower, when they owned this land. Do you think Chinese people want to go back to working hard on the railroads and living in cities underground? Do Japanese people want to go back to living in internment camps? White have-nots, are you ready to again, have most of the good opportunities go back to the wealthy Whites? Gay people, are you ready to go back into the closet? So, again I ask, who benefits from America being great, again? Come on, think hard, I'm sure the answer will eventually dawn upon you.

For those of you who only reply is, "Well if you don't like it, leave it", there simply are no words for you. I will say this once and for all, I love America. Not for her greatness but for her potential to be great. America has never been great to all of its citizens. Brave soldiers have fought all over the world because of the potential of America's greatness. That's not saying that for a young country we haven't made great strides. We do a lot of things better than the rest of the world. However, loving fellow Americans who might have different skin color, religious beliefs, or may be of a different gender, have always been a thorn in the side of America's potential greatness. And don't forget to throw in the several other "-isms" and prejudices that keep many groups of people under thumb. To be honest, the reason we never seem to attain positive progress in these hideous "-ism" areas is because of that very, "love it or leave it" mentality. Ultimately this type of thinking warrants no real plan of action. When it comes to social change, no action, always produces no social change.

America is her people. America can only be great if her people are great. People can't behave badly in America and still call it great. However, because there are some great people, most of them powerless, America has only the potential to be great. If, or when, the people of America decide to go from potential to reality and treat every man, woman, and child in America with respect and basic human dignity, then the world will truly see the greatness of America. Sadly, I don't think that will ever happen because of the "Gap Tool". It will be sent to separate us if we show any signs of coming together as a people. The last thing the minority super wealthy want to see is the majority non-wealthy thinking and communicating as a caring group of people. So, the "Gap Tool" is used, to keep people apart, to give a few of the non-wealthy, a taste of wealth. This gives many of the majority-poor a false sense of hope. It appeases us for a while.

The "Gap Tool" keeps doing its job by widening and exploiting the differences between groups of people in America. What's interesting is how many people can't see the "Gap Tool" at work. Like I mentioned before, if someone is talking about making American great AGAIN, that's a clue to everyone who America hasn't ever been great to in the first place. It's also code for: we want things to be like they used to be when people of color, women and the poor, knew their places.

I think we have reached the when someone's only purpose for using the "Gap Tool" is to watch America burn! So, America hear me and hear me well, beware of whom you elect to lead this potentially great nation. Following a Pied Piper down a dusty road of hatred and bigotry will take America to hellish existence to which there is no return. Most Americans will fight back against hatred in a suit. And while our civil war rages, like all the great empires before us, our enemies lay in wait, to defeat the once potential greatness of America.

The Idea

There's a person who has sent me articles about how the Irish were at one time persecuted. The message this person has been trying to send to me is, "you don't see the Irish blaming their problems on racism". I've been hoping that a light would pop on in this person's mind, helping him/her to see the big difference between the Irish's situation and the situation of being a person of color, especially Black, in America. It doesn't appear that any such light will pop on. So, I will explain why the persecution of most groups of people in this country was and is, so much different than that of Black people. And for the record, Black people and people of color do not complain to receive your damn pity. And guess what, if the racism against Black people stopped, immediately you'd see some differences in attitude. But it would take a generation or two to undo generational poverty, hatred and the mental mindset that comes with generational racism. I would love to live one day of my life and not feel or experience or read what the system of racism and hatred has done to another Black person, or any other person of color. Do I think what I write will change this person's attitude about why racism against Black people in this country, became and continues to be different from the persecution of most, if not all, other groups of people in this country? No, I don't.

First, let me again acknowledge that there's no doubt that every group of people on this planet has had their time under persecution. But in this country, the outcome of racism and hatred towards Black people has had and continues to have a lasting, profound effect, not only on Black people, but on everyone in this country. Forgive me for sounding a little bit annoyed, but having to still deal with the topic of hatred and racism gets old.

Some time ago a group of people came to this already occupied land and claimed it for their own. Many of them came from different parts of Europe (What one thing did most of them had in common?).

Some came as free men, and some came as indentured servants. There was so much land and so much work that needed to be done. How would they proceed? They didn't have enough indentured servants. Besides most of the indentured servants escaped and were able to hide in plain sight (I wonder why they're able to do that). The Europeans decided to enslave the Indians to do their hard labor, but that idea just didn't work. The first reason it didn't work was because the Indians knew the land better than they did and could escape. After all it was their country. Second, a significant number of Indians died from diseases that the Europeans brought to this country. And finally, the Indians decided that they would rather die than become slaves.

So, the people from Europe had to come up with another idea. They noticed that a few of their citizens, who had made the long journey with them, had uniquely dark skin. So, they came up with "the idea". They heard of some other dark-skinned people. So, they went and stole these dark-skinned people, mostly from a place called Africa. They had an "idea" to enslave them. Sometimes a greedy chief would sell some of his own people, but it was cheaper for the White man to steal and kidnap slaves. And for good measure they even enslaved some of their dark-skinned countrymen who were formerly freemen or indentured servants. The Europeans instituted a brand of slavery that was different than the indentured servant system. It was mean and brutal. Mentally they convinced themselves that the dark-skinned people were less than human. Doing this allowed them to physically and mentally mistreat the slaves without feeling guilty. They even preached the righteousness of beating slaves in their churches.

Thousands of miles from Africa, there was nothing the Africans could do. They didn't know the land, the language, and because of their dark skin, they stuck-out and most of the time they didn't get very far when they ran away. For slave owners it was a simple system. If you had black skin, you surely belonged to someone. However, some of the dark-skinned women began to have babies and those babies weren't so dark (I wonder who was having sex with the dark women). At the same time the beatings, raping and the negative stereotyping of the Black male slave continued. Yes, they raped Black male slaves. In some sad ways the effects of these rapes, beatings and negative stereotyping affects Black folk until this day.

When slavery had done all the ugly damage it could do, some guy named Lincoln was instrumental in getting rid of the institution of slavery. However, it accelerated the institution of racism. Not having black slaves to beat up on and mistreat, caused many of the different groups of Europeans to fight amongst themselves. Then one of them said, we all have the same color skin, let's call ourselves White people and we will own and run this country. In fact, let's make a law prohibiting people with colored skin to come here until we outnumber them by so much, that we can never be overtaken. The original United States Naturalization Law of March 26, 1790 (1 Stat. 103) provided the first rules to be followed by the United States in the granting of national citizenship. This law limited naturalization to immigrants who were free white persons of good character. It thus excluded American Indians, indentured servants, slaves, free blacks, and Asians. It also provided for citizenship for the children of U.S. citizens born abroad but specified that the right of citizenship did "not descend to persons whose fathers have never been resident in the United States." It specifies that such children "shall be considered as natural-born citizens," the only US statute ever to use the term. The effects of this law can be seen today. White people by far, outnumber everyone else in this country.

A lot of people from white-skinned countries come to America, drop their accent, change their names and receive the benefits of being White. People of color cannot receive the complete benefits of this country, by changing our names. Most of us are born and raised here so the only accent we have are the ones from places in America, such as the South, Texas or the East or West Coast. The fact that people of color can't come to this country and hide like other groups of people with white skin can, is one of the reasons why people of color and especially Black people, STILL have to deal with racism and hatred on a daily basis. Englishmen, the Polish,

Irishmen, Italians and any other white-skinned group of people, although they shouldn't have to, do have the option of dropping their accents and changing their names to blend in and share the American dream. In the last 30-40 years, white skinned Bosnian people (there are darker skinned Bosnians) have been the latest group of people able to come to this country and blend in. A lot of people of color work hard and still have to deal with hatred and racism. When was the last time, in this country an Englishman, the Polish, Irishmen, Italians and any other white-skinned group of people had to deal with system of hatred and racism, by corporations, the educational system and law enforcement? No one is saying that many White people haven't worked hard for what they have, but to really believe that the system in American wasn't designed so that White people could succeed easier than people of color, you must be living on a river in Egypt called denial. However, I do understand; everyone one wants to believe that they pulled themselves up by their own bootstraps. This makes it easy for the so-called self-made man, to look down on any group of people living under the hell of ongoing hatred and racism. He will always ask, why don't people of color and Black people just stop complaining and do like my people did? I'll say this to that: we just didn't think of "the idea" of slavery before you.

The Other Racism

Back in the day, slave owners classified the Negro as part animal, sub-human, and not worthy of being educated. This allowed these slave owners, many of them forefathers of this country, to clear their minds of guilt and any type of redemption from God. This misguided justification to classify the Negro and Indians as less than human and savages, was all they needed to execute a plan that would last for generations. This plan was designed to give and retain power to people with white skin, forever.

Thankfully, today most people don't believe Blacks are less than human, Indians are savages, or Mexicans are lazy. However, racism isn't perpetrated effectively by the few extremely hateful people, screaming in the faces of people of color. The key to the success of racism are the people sitting on the fence, doing nothing to stop racism. Sure, these people may think racism is wrong; they may even show sadness when a violent, racist act happens to someone. But, without question, the most damage done by racism, happens when everyday normal people don't take any action against racism.

So how do we start to undo racism? First, know that racism isn't a trait we were born with. We were taught to hate. As a fighter of racism, you must know and understand that racism has to be undone systematically, just as purposefully as it was done. Racism will not take care of itself. We must fight. And to be totally honest, we need White allies. Racism will not be destroyed without White people who "get it". Telling people of color how sad you are about what is going on does nothing to stop what's going on in this country. Go look at civil rights marches from the 60's and you'll see there were White people who "got it". Many of them were hit and injured as they marched alongside people of color.

Second, just because a person isn't overtly perpetrating hateful acts on people, doesn't mean they aren't possibly racist. More and more racism uses its power to control groups of people. A lot of times racism is covert. Usually overt racism comes before covert racism. Overt racism is used to instill physical fear into a group of people. Once the brutality of overt racism is fought and condemned by the masses, including White people, covert racism usually kicks in. The power group stops kicking the powerless group in the ass physically but begins to kick their minds. This mind-kicking becomes like a mental beating. It is designed to instill a sense of hopelessness. It is designed to make the powerless feel less than human, or less than a man.

Let me take a detour for a second. We see this very situation of feeling less than human or less than a man, going on around this country now. People of color and especially Black men must act almost childlike, so we won't get shot during a routine traffic stop. We are now having to teach our young sons to kowtow to mostly White police forces. In my mind, a traffic stop for young unarmed Black men is like a slave walking on eggshells so that the master won't whip him again. Of course, that isn't the case with every policeman, at every traffic stop. But I don't know one responsible father or mother who has said this happens so infrequently that my son doesn't need to worry about it. We've seen enough killings of unarmed Black men, that we to have to believe that any of us can be killed at any time. The guy who killed the policemen in Dallas is dead. He did a cowardly, horrible thing and he got what he deserved. So, isn't it fair to ask and expect the policemen who killed the last two Black men, will have to answer for what they did?

Okay, back to fighting racism. Third, educate yourself by reading and learning what racism is about. Most of the time people repeat things they've heard. Even when true facts are used to rebuke their lies, they stick with the lies they've heard. Most Pied Pipers know that the average person wants to be told what to think. As a fighter of racism, you must understand that these are the people you're up against. So, in order to enlighten them, you must be able to guide them past their "right to their opinion". You must know that just because people have a right to their opinion, it doesn't mean their opinion is worth a damn. So, know your facts. Know who's really abusing the welfare system by knowing statistically, who's really on welfare. There is a lot of White on White crime, but we don't hear about it on the news. But, ask victims if White on White crime exists.

Lastly, watch out for Uncle Tom and Aunt Bessie. These are people of color who are wolves in sheep clothing. We know about the famous ones, because we see them on television. They blame people of color for poverty and the racist things that happen to people of color. Television host Wendy Williams played the Aunt Bessie when she declared that Historical Black Colleges and Universities as racist, and The NAACP as being pretty much racist. However, veteran television newsperson Roland Martin, using knowledge and facts, put Wendy in her place. She apologized the week Roland was a guest on her show. Don't be fooled, her apology probably had something to do with losing sponsors, which means the network losing money. These Uncle Tom and Aunt Bessie of today got their roles from slavery. There were Negro slaves who survived by telling on the other slaves. They function pretty much the same way today. They want to be known as the "good Black, Brown, Red or Yellow". In any case, watch out for them.

After we get through this overt phase of racism, we'll have to deal with the covert aspect of racism. These different aspects of racism come in cycles, much like the season of the year. Maybe one day, we'll begin to understand that there is only one race, the human race. We are all people. We all live, and we all die. No one group of people is so superior that they live forever. Give yourself the gift of love. Then, share your love with everyone you can.